WILBRAHAM PUBLIC LIBRARY

WILBRAHAM PUBLIC LIBRARY

Creating Bonsai

Joe Davies

Creating Bonsai

Joe Davies

Trafalgar Square Publishing

For Lesley

I think that I shall never see
a poem lovely as a tree.

Joyce Kilmer

Printed in Hong Kong for the Publisher

First published in the United States of America in 1996 by
Trafalgar Square Publishing North Pomfret, Vermont 05053

Originally published in Great Britain 1995
by BT Batsford, Ltd

© Joe Davies 1995

All rights reserved. No part of this publication may be
reproduced in any form or by any means without the
permission of the publisher

Library of Congress Catalog Card Number 95 - 62446
ISBN 1-57076-055-1

10 9 8 7 6 5 4 3 2 1

Contents

Preface

Here is a new approach to teaching the skills and methods of creating and caring for Bonsai trees. Mankind has a natural affinity with trees, and part of the fascination of Bonsai is that through it you can enjoy the splendour of trees within a garden of any size. The miniaturization of trees is not a difficult task, but to create a Bonsai that actually looks like a small tree does require an insight into the key elements of design and shaping techniques. Fashioning beautiful Bonsai is within the capability of most people - it is a skill that can be taught. But, as with many other skills, one's abilities improve with practice and experience.

The core of the book, the Projects Section, demonstrates the creation of eight different Bonsai trees from basic materials. The detailed step-by-step coverage of each creation guides the enthusiast through all the techniques required. The Bonsai process is explained and simplified so that the reader may have the satisfaction of creating his or her own Bonsai trees inexpensively and with confidence.

Sections on design, shaping techniques, materials and care, as well as a species guide, complete the picture: the requirements for successful Bonsai growing are clearly set out. The key aspects are reinforced by inspirational case studies of Bonsai created by the author.

Introduction

The true origin of Bonsai is uncertain. The Romans, Persians and Indians all grew trees in containers, but it was the Chinese who first practised the craft of Bonsai as we know it today. In the late Middle Ages, as trade between China and Japan flourished, Bonsai was taken up by the Japanese, who adopted and adapted it to their own culture, and were the first to develop it into a true art form in its own right. Today, Japan is often perceived as the mother nation of Bonsai.

Over the last hundred years the appreciation of Bonsai has spread world-wide and Bonsai are now grown and enjoyed in almost every country. Europe and the USA are now major centres for the growing of Bonsai trees, with an ever-increasing store of skills and knowledge. Indeed, while the basis of the art form still lies with its oriental origins, and while the technical skill of the professional Japanese Bonsai growers still exceeds that of the West, it might be said that their style has become overly regimented, obsessed with rules - with a resultant loss of spontaneity.

The goal of this book is to bring the creation of Bonsai within the reach of anyone with the desire to learn it. The book has long been an ambition of mine and one of the hardest tasks I have ever attempted. I hope my enthusiasm and love of the subject is apparent in the pages which follow.

The book has been inspired by the many requests I have received over the years from my students and customers, both to show in detail the techniques of creating Bonsai and to explain the WHYs of the subject. I believe this can only be achieved by comprehensive pictorial coverage of each stage of the process. Everything in this book is based on my own experience - it is a practical book, not a theoretical one. My approach is to simplify, and to demonstrate that Bonsai is a far easier subject to understand than is generally imagined.

This is a book about *doing* and, on occasions, getting one's hands dirty. My task will have been successful if you, the reader, are encouraged to try to create Bonsai yourself - if I have managed to engender sufficient confidence for you to tackle the projects.

There is an old Chinese proverb that nicely sums up my philosophy: 'I hear and I forget, I see and I remember, I do and I understand'. Do have a go at the projects: they are easier than they may first appear, and from them you will gain two most important things - understanding and satisfaction.

1

The craft of Bonsai

A maple Bonsai with beautiful red leaves. Find out how to create this Bonsai in Project 1.

What is a Bonsai?

The literal translation of the Japanese word 'Bonsai' is 'potted tree'. However, as with many words translated from one language to another, much of the inherent sense has been lost in the translation. Just planting a tree in a pot does not make it a Bonsai.

The pastime of Bonsai encompasses many skills - horticulture, manual craftsmanship, a sense of design. It is the combined application of these skills that produces an image of a tree in the wild that may be truly called a Bonsai.

There is no ultimate answer to the question 'what is a Bonsai?' as the term means slightly different things to everybody. However, a good working definition, the one that this book is founded upon, is: 'A Bonsai is a living, miniaturized tree, planted in a container, that exhibits the natural beauty of a tree growing in the wild.'

Bonsai myths and misconceptions

Bonsai has been the subject of many misconceptions. Understanding these is fundamental in learning how to create and maintain Bonsai.

A rock planting of Ezo Spruce, imported into the UK from Japan in the early 1960s. Now over 60 years old this Bonsai has had a succession of owners - all of whom have tended and cared for it.

Bonsai is an expensive pastime
Untrue. Purchasing mature Bonsai from nurseries can be expensive, but creating one's own Bonsai is relatively inexpensive and gives great satisfaction.

Bonsai are kept small by mistreating them - the technique is cruel to trees
Untrue. On the contrary - a Bonsai tree is well-watered and fertilized to ensure its continued good health. The techniques of Bonsai are no more cruel than those of any other horticultural endeavour.

Bonsai are special, natural dwarf trees
Untrue. Bonsai trees are species from the forest, plain and mountainside - not genetically dwarf species. They are kept small by the application of Bonsai procedures and techniques.

Bonsai are kept small by cutting off their roots
Untrue. Bonsai are kept small by pruning their branches and twigs. Bonsai are regularly root-pruned for one reason only - that is, they become pot-bound and the roots must be reduced to allow fresh soil to be added. A pot-bound plant cannot absorb water or nutrients properly and will eventually die.

Bonsai are wired to keep them small
Untrue. Bonsai have wire applied to their branches, and sometimes trunks, so that these limbs may be placed into different positions. Once the limb is set in the new position the wire is removed. The wire shapes, but should not constrict.

Bonsai with wire on are unfinished

Untrue. A Bonsai is a continually growing and changing object and in that sense it can never be 'finished'. It is regularly re-shaped to accommodate changes in its growth and size. Providing the wiring is neat and appropriate it is quite acceptable to exhibit Bonsai that are wired.

An English elm Bonsai grown in the style of a mature elm tree. The initial creation of this Bonsai took a short time, but building up the detailed tracery of twigs took many more years. Since the demise of the once-flourishing elm in the British landscape, this may be the only time one sees a 'mature' elm.

The leaves on a Bonsai are not small so it cannot be called a Bonsai

Untrue. Although some reduction in the size of the leaves occurs through the Bonsai process, the leaf size is not of prime importance on medium-sized and large Bonsai. Species with small leaves are usually chosen when creating small Bonsai.

Bonsai must be from Japan

Untrue. A Bonsai is a miniaturized tree, its origin matters not (in fact many imported Bonsai now originate in Korea, China, Taiwan and Israel). A Bonsai created in the UK, Europe, USA or anywhere else is just as valid as one from the Orient.

Inexpensive hedging trees, such as this bundle of hornbeam stock plants obtained from a nursery, are transformed into a Bonsai in just a few hours. Simply follow the techniques contained in this book.

Bonsai are kept indoors

Untrue. While some species that are now imported require frost-free conditions and are subsequently sold as Indoor Bonsai, the reality is that all trees require high light levels and a good air flow - conditions which are not found inside the home. In addition, the vagaries of humidity, and pollution from gas boilers, cooking, smoking and open fires are all unsuitable for keeping Bonsai in the home on a long-term basis. Bonsai are not house plants: they require an exterior environment. It is far better to have several Bonsai and rotate them in turn, so that each may be enjoyed in the home for a few days at a time.

Bonsai are grown from seeds and cuttings; creating a Bonsai takes a long time

Untrue. While Bonsai are sometimes grown from seedlings, they are more usually created from existing stock plants obtained from a nursery or garden centre. The basic Bonsai shape and structure is formed very quickly from the raw material; then the fine detail, such as the tracery of twigs, is built up over subsequent years.

Bonsai are small - just a few inches tall

Untrue. While some Bonsai are small, the majority are over 30 cm. (1 ft.) tall. It is easier to create and maintain larger Bonsai than small ones. The size is unimportant provided the image is credible as a tree.

Bonsai are difficult to look after

Untrue. Bonsai grown from native species are no more difficult to look after than any other exterior potted plant. The main inhibition to the expansion of Bonsai as a hobby is the sale of poor-quality, mass-produced 'indoor' Bonsai. The appearance of these Bonsai is seductive, but they are often difficult species for the novice to maintain - they have been chosen to sell on their attractiveness rather than their ease of maintenance.

Buying a Bonsai is the best way to enjoy the hobby

Untrue. How is one to look after a Bonsai without the knowledge and understanding of the techniques for maintaining its shape and health? Few Bonsai hobbyists have collections consisting entirely of purchased trees for this very reason. Also, there is much satisfaction to be gained by having accomplished the creation process oneself.

To grow Bonsai successfully one needs a knowledge of Oriental arts and sciences

Untrue. Following the techniques and projects contained in this book will enable you to practise and enjoy the craft of Bonsai, and to develop the understanding and skills required to keep your Bonsai trees in good health.

Bonsai design

When you are creating a Bonsai tree, there are several considerations to be addressed. However, the most important consideration is that the final appearance of a Bonsai should appeal to the grower - if the owner of the Bonsai is unhappy with the shape then the design has somehow failed.

The following sections give advice and guidance on the aesthetic aspects of Bonsai design and the techniques that will help you to create Bonsai. But you should not lose sight of the fact that the 'completed' Bonsai must have personal appeal.

Trees in nature

Natural trees are our role models when designing Bonsai. A tree is composed of several elements: roots, trunk, branches, twigs and leaves. Understanding how these elements combine to tell us whether the tree is old or young will help us to design Bonsai trees that look natural.

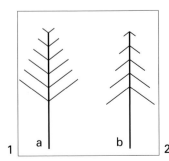 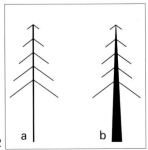 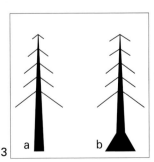

In each diagram which image looks older ... A or B?
In each diagram B gives a stronger impression of age.

13

Mature trees provide inspiration for the aspiring Bonsai designer.

Diagram 1. Branches pointing skyward are indicative of youth (a). The tree grows strongly towards the sunlight while it is young. As it ages, the branches grow larger and heavier, and gravity pulls them towards the ground (b). Older trees invariably have drooping branches with many smaller, secondary branches and twigs. This density of branches and twigs is known as 'ramification'.

Diagram 2. A tall, slender trunk is the mark of a young tree (a). Each part of the trunk thickens relative to the amount of growth above it (b), hence the trunk is thicker nearer the ground. This is called 'taper'.

Diagram 3. Stable spreading roots are the sign of a tree that has developed a firm base and has withstood the vagaries of weather and time (b). A younger tree lacks this root buttress (a), referred to in Bonsai terms as 'rootage'. A rounded top (b) is typical of a tree at maturity. It has reached its maximum height and the vigour of the tree has been redistributed throughout its whole. A younger specimen exhibits a typical 'Christmas Tree' habit (a), with the main vigour expressed in growing upwards. In Bonsai, a domed top or 'apex' is desirable.

A sturdy base of strong rootage, a trunk that tapers, branches with well-defined ramification and a rounded apex all contribute to an appearance of maturity and age. When we see a tree, these are the attributes that tell us it is old. These characteristics are used by the Bonsai designer as building blocks to produce a convincing image of an old, fully grown tree, but in miniature.

These, then, are the ground rules of good Bonsai design: derive inspiration by studying the trees that surround us, then reproduce those key elements when shaping the raw material into a Bonsai tree.

Trees come in many different shapes: some are tall and graceful, others are short and powerful. But they are all trees, and as such are valid images for the Bonsai grower to use as models. This is the most important principle of Bonsai design. Trees surround our lives - in the countryside, in books and magazines, on TV and films. There is no lack of examples to study and to copy.

Mature trees are the role models for the Bonsai grower. The strong root buttress, tapering trunk and dense twiggy branch canopy seen here are those aspects that are copied when designing Bonsai.

Bonsai styles

Bonsai trees have been traditionally categorized into five major styles, depending on the angle and shape of the trunk. The Japanese term for each style is indicated after the more common title.

Formal upright (*Chokkan*) – a vertical trunk which must have well defined taper and be absolutely straight.
Slanting (*Shakan*) – the trunk may be curved or straight but must slant at an angle.
Semi-cascade (*Han-kengai*) – the trunk leans over to the level of the rim of the pot.
Cascade (*Kengai*) – the trunk grows downwards below the pot.
Informal upright (*Moyogi*) – trunks that do not conform to the previous four categories. (In practice, this particular style accounts for the majority of Bonsai.)

These styles reflect the classical Japanese origins of Bonsai. It is sufficient for the student of Bonsai to be aware of this classification system, without attempting to subjugate their material so that it fits a particular style. There are many variations emanating from the five basic styles, and also styles that do not fit within the formal classification system (such as forest and group plantings). The following styles represent those that are most commonly encountered.

Windswept (*Fukinagashi*) – a derivative of the Slanting style. The style reflects the history of a tree from a windy location, often with one-sided growth and a trunk

The classification of Bonsai trees derives from the many differing styles of tree found in nature. An ancient yew growing on a wall of a ruined monastery – its roots flow over and down the wall. Its mirror in Bonsai, shown below, is a sycamore with its roots firmly clasping a stone – not surprisingly this style is referred to as 'root over rock'.

16

that slants at an angle. Not the easiest style to create, as the diagonal appearance of the trunk line tends to make the Bonsai appear unstable. This style needs good rootage and relatively few, well-placed branches to counteract the inherent appearance of instability. However, when accomplished successfully, this is one of the most dramatic of all Bonsai styles. (This and the Literati style are the author's favourites.)

Broom (*Hokidachi*) – a variation of the Formal upright style. The branches emanate usually from the top of the trunk to form a very natural image. Many people perceive this style as the most 'tree-like' of all Bonsai, but it takes experience and dedication to create this style, and many years to build up the required twiggy ramification of the branches.

Literati (*Bunjungi*) – a style derived from ancient Chinese scroll drawings. A very free-form Bonsai that most succinctly captures the Oriental view of nature. The trunk line usually curves and twists, giving a flowing feeling of movement. The foliage is minimal.

Weeping style – A derivative of any of the five main classical styles. The trunk shape can be of any form, but all the branches flow downwards in the manner of a riverside weeping willow.

Root over rock (*Sekijoju*) – a single Bonsai planted on a rock, with the roots exposed and flowing down the rock into the container. The exposed roots need to clasp the rock firmly for this style to appear natural rather than contrived.

Landscape planting (usually referred to by its Chinese term, *Penjing*) – re-creation of a landscape scene in miniature with rocks, stones, small Bonsai and mosses. This style is popular in China where the cultural preference is for a more natural appearance to their Bonsai.

Driftwood style (*Sharimiki*) – large areas of white dead wood abound, which give an impression of great age. The inspiration for this style is the ancient junipers and pines that are found growing at high altitudes and have struggled for survival for many centuries.

Exposed root style (*Neagari*) – As the name suggests, thick roots are exposed. Derived from the riverside trees that one sees with much of the soil surrounding their roots washed away. Can be slightly odd to Western eyes; more popular in China than Japan.

Forest group style (*Yose-ue*) – A style that is readily achieved and can produce convincing results from initially unspectacular material. Anything from two individual trees up to twenty or more.

Many of the traditional styles of Bonsai are represented here, in a display of part of the author's collection.

Root connected styles – The Raft style simulates a fallen trunk: the branches have grown upwards and appear as individual trees. If the original trunk is straight, the style is referred to as Straight Line Raft (*Ikadabuki*); if the original trunk is curved and twisted it is known as Sinuous Raft (*Netsunanari*). An often-seen variant of the Raft style is the twin-trunk Bonsai (*Sokan*). Clump style (*Kabudachi*) has several trunks emanating from a single root source, and has the initial appearance of a group or forest planting.

Photographs of the majority of these styles are contained within this book, and it is pertinent for the Bonsai student to understand the basis of these main styles. However, deriving enjoyment and pleasure from the initial creation, and subsequent refinement, of a Bonsai is the key, and moulding this design so that it conforms to a particular classification is of less importance.

A literati-style Scots pine over 50 years old.

Bonsai design in practice

The maturity of trees in the wild comes with age. In Bonsai, the impression of age is brought about by applying the Bonsai creator's skill to certain aspects of the tree's structure and appearance, namely to its rootage and branches, to create effects by means of taper and an appropriately shaped apex. In this way, a Bonsai can evoke a feeling of great age while it is still relatively young, and in years to come it will improve even further. If we are to create Bonsai that meet the criteria outlined below, then we must start with material that already has some of the required elements.

A good root buttress and taper are the most important basic considerations in selecting raw material from stock plants to create Bonsai trees, as these attributes are difficult to achieve without specialized techniques, or waiting for many years. If a potential Bonsai has these desired attributes, then the shaping process and further growth will create the rounded apex and ramified branch structure.

When you design Bonsai there are three key criteria:
miniaturization;
visual perspective;
health and aftercare.

Miniaturization

At only 3 in. (7 cm.) tall this Bonsai is at the extreme of miniaturization, yet it has the hallmark of a mature tree. Eight years of patient work have transformed a cutting into a genuine Bonsai.

A Bonsai is a miniature tree, not a dwarf tree. A dwarf tree is a genetically distinct tree, whose natural habit is slow growth and reduced maximum size. The species of tree and shrub predominantly used in Bonsai are those of the forest, plain and mountain, which would achieve a full, natural size if planted out away from the Bonsai pot.

In nature, miniaturization occurs naturally in some environments, such as at high altitude, where ultra-violet light levels may be one of the factors involved; short growing seasons and shallow soil may also make a contribution. In Bonsai, miniaturization is achieved by two basic techniques - pruning and root restriction, although pruning is the prime technique. Throughout the life of a Bonsai it is continually pruned, both to shape it and also to maintain its size. Root restriction also has a miniaturizing effect - the less space the roots have to grow, the smaller will be the total size of the root system. In any plant the branch structure will grow in proportion to the amount of water and nutrients supplied by the root system, and thus a small root ball results in a small tree.

Another aspect of successful miniaturization is reduction of the overall number of branches. A mature oak tree may have many branches and up to half-a-million leaves. There is no way this abundance of branches and leaves may be reproduced in miniature: the leaves would be microscopic in size! Rather, the Bonsai grower reduces the number of branches and leaves to create an illusion of a larger tree. This is the method by which a landscape artist represents a tree in a painting - creating the impression of a tree by reducing the number of its individual components and emphasizing those which remain. This is the basic technique adopted in many of the projects within this book: when excess foliage is removed, so that the trunk and junctions between the trunk and branches are exposed, a changed appearance results that is altogether more tree-like.

20

A beech Bonsai growing in the style of a mature tree in the countryside. An artist emphasizes the key elements of a tree and does not paint every branch and leaf - the same technique, a form of 'impressionism', is used by the Bonsai grower who miniaturizes the whole image by emphasizing those same key elements.

The miniaturizing effects of keeping a tree in a pot will also reduce the size of the leaves after many years. It is a difficult task to reduce leaf size permanently in some trees, such as horse chestnut, so these are rarely used in Bonsai. More commonly, species with smallish leaves are selected in the first place.

How large should a Bonsai be?

A Bonsai can be any size from a few inches or centimetres tall through to a giant of a metre-and-a-half - all these sizes are acceptable as Bonsai. The size is unimportant: the credibility of its image as a mature tree is the vital point. Size is relative: for example the largest trees in the world, the Giant Sequoia of California, grow to 367 ft. (110 m.) in height. A Bonsai sequoia of 3 ft. (1 m.) in height is tiny in comparison. In practice, especially if one is new to Bonsai, a height of 12-24 in. (30-60 cm.) is preferred. Smaller than 12 in. (30 cm.), and there are difficulties in physically wiring and pruning such a small object. Larger than 24 in. (60 cm.), and the Bonsai can lack portability. In addition, from a purely visual point of view, a small Bonsai has to be almost perfect to be credible; faults in larger Bonsai are less apparent.

Bonsai may be large or small. Although this azalea is little more than a rooted cutting, it is dwarfed by the trunk of a mature beech Bonsai.

Visual perspective

A Bonsai has a front and a back. That is, it has been designed to be viewed from a particular angle. When creating a Bonsai from raw material, the front is normally chosen as the side which has the best root buttress and will give the most pleasing appearance. If there is a choice of 'fronts', then the one where the branches are best-placed is chosen.

Existing branches are pruned so that the back branches are longer than those at the front. This gives a very stable perspective when viewed from the front. If the situation is reversed and the back branches are shorter than the front, then the tree has an unbalanced appearance. In addition, the trunk should always tilt very slightly towards the viewer; again this balances the whole design.

These subtleties in the placement and the length of branches or the angle of the trunk may appear initially to be very minor but, in fact, they are important. They are among the 'tricks of the trade' that often separate a quality Bonsai from a lesser one.

A Bonsai, although intended to be viewed from one particular side, is a three-dimensional object and as such requires branches at the front, sides and back. When training a Bonsai it is a good idea periodically to look downwards at the branch

22

A delightful elm Bonsai. When viewed from the side the back branches are longer than the front ones, and the trunk leans very slightly forward - both of these design elements enhance the visual perspective of the image.

structure from above. The branches should flow out in all directions without crossing or obscuring one another. Crossing branches (although natural in some species) look wrong on a Bonsai which has fewer branches. If branches obscure each other when viewed from above, it is likely that the lower branch will get shaded by the branch above, causing the lower one to weaken and eventually die through lack of light.

There is another occasion in Bonsai when perspective plays an important part: with a group planting, where a forest scene is recreated. In this case the tallest and largest trees are generally placed at the front of the planting and smaller ones at the rear (as demonstrated in Project 3). This is what we see when we look at a forest - the closest trees appear the largest and those in the distance are smaller. If the small trees are placed in the front then they merely look smaller and younger than the others.

Trees are rarely symmetrical in appearance - very little in Nature is. When looking at a Bonsai from any angle, but in particular from the front, the branch structures on each side of the trunk should not be mirror images of one other. This difference, or imbalance, is called 'asymmetry'. If a Bonsai looks symmetrical it will not look real - it will appear 'man-made'. So attention should be given to ensuring that any Bonsai design has a degree of asymmetry.

Health and aftercare considerations

It is all very well to produce a stunning Bonsai, but if it dies later as a result of the design process then your efforts will have been to no avail. The health of the tree is paramount. Assuming the raw material is in good health to start with, then the major cause of mortality is the inability to recover the functions of the root system - due to either excess root pruning or inappropriate aftercare.

After styling and repotting, these Bonsai have been placed under a bench. This is an excellent aftercare environment - protected from the worst of the weather and sun, but with adequate light and air.

Removal of part of a root system as a preliminary to fitting a Bonsai into a container has to be done with care. It is possible to remove a portion of the root system, although much depends on the species of tree, the time of year, and whether the roots that are removed are serving any branches that are also removed – in any event, an appropriate part of the upper part of the tree has to be removed at the same time. Removal of a large portion of the root system is best performed as the tree awakens from its winter dormant period in early to late spring. The tree is at its strongest at this time of year as it is preparing to release its stored energy into producing the new year's growth.

The root pruning undertaken during the Bonsai process does give a tremendous shock to the tree. It will be resilient enough to survive that shock and to remain healthy, as long as sensible aftercare is given.

After repotting it must be watered-in thoroughly and then placed in a frost-free environment that has good air flow - this prevents fungus attacks, such as mildew. If it is an evergreen or has already sprouted leaves then good light levels are required for it to perform photosynthesis. It needs to be kept frost-free as freezing of the soil may damage the cut root-ends. Positions such as on the porch of a house, or underneath a greenhouse bench, are good locations. The branches and twigs should be misted as often as is practical - several times a day if possible, daily as a minimum. Misting helps the production of new buds on deciduous trees and many evergreens are able to absorb water through their leaves. This helps to keep up the internal moisture-content of the tree while it is redeveloping its root system. The soil is not watered again until it starts to dry out: this drying is an indication that the roots have recovered and are taking up water again. If excess water is given during this aftercare period there is danger that the root ends will rot. Fertilizer is not given until the root system has recovered and the tree is growing and healthy. Normally this will be after 2–3 months.

Methods of shaping Bonsai

To produce a miniaturized version of a mature tree, a Bonsai must be shaped. The Bonsai grower is merely refining, improving upon the natural elements of the raw material, but one cannot achieve successful Bonsai without a degree of boldness. There is a saying 'no pain, no gain'; in this case the pain is one's own in making assertive decisions whilst shaping a Bonsai. Bonsai have to be handled and shaped sensitively, but boldly.

Wiring

This is probably the best-known of all Bonsai shaping techniques. Originally, in China, Bonsai were shaped mainly by pruning alone. Then weights were added to branches to lower them, and various complex systems were used for tying small lengths of wood to the branches to alter their position. In modern times, these methods have evolved, and now a specialized wire is used to alter the position of branches and even to shape the trunk itself.

Bonsai wire comes in thicknesses, or gauges, from 0.5 mm to 6 mm. It is made of either annealed copper or aluminium, though the latter is more commonly available and easier to use. The thicker the wire the greater the holding power. You need experience to know exactly which gauge of wire to use in any given circumstance, but it is quickly learnt.

Wiring techniques and tips

Use either proprietary Bonsai wire or a suitable substitute (copper electrical wire may be used).

Wire outwards from the trunk. Start by using thick wire for the branches, then thinner wire for the smaller sub-branches and twigs. Try not to cross wires on top of each other as this reduces their holding power.

Apply common sense with the tightness of the wire. If wire is too tightly applied it will scar the bark; too loosely and it will not hold and the re-positioned branch will spring back to its original position.

Apply the wire evenly in spirals, with the loops not too close and not too far apart.

Wire is best removed by cutting it with wire cutters. This prevents any damage to the tree from your physical efforts at unravelling the wire (removing wire intact and attempting to re-use it is a false economy). If the wire has already scarred the branch and left gouges it should still be removed as carefully as possible and the 'cuts' treated with wound sealant.

Wiring should be neat and the spirals evenly spaced - not too close and not too far apart. Thick branches may need more than one piece of wire; in this case (the Yew in Case Study 3) multiple wires are positioned close together for maximum holding power.

Always anchor the wire firmly. This is best achieved by using a single piece of wire for two adjacent branches, so that one anchors the other. Experiment and practice this wiring technique in a redundant branch.

How long should the wire be left on? In practice this can be any duration between a few weeks and a few years. Wire on a weeping willow may be removed in just a few weeks; on an old pine tree it may take several years for the branch to be set in its new position. The wire should always be removed before it cuts into the bark. If the limb moves back to its original position then it is wired again.

Pruning

A Bonsai is pruned throughout its life. There are three stages of development of the Bonsai from raw material to completion, each requiring a different pruning technique.

1. Defining the structure

When a Bonsai is first shaped from raw material (such as a stock plant from a nursery) the branch structure needs to be defined. Excess branches, ones that are overly thick and those in the 'wrong' places, are removed. They are removed altogether and cut back cleanly to the trunk. This is usually done with a specialized tool called 'branch pruners' (see page 33).

2. Encouraging inner budding

The branch structure having been laid down, the next efforts are to encourage the branches to produce growth all along their length. Often (particularly with stock plants) the interior of the tree has been shaded and the inner growth has died resulting in a 'lollipop' appearance to the branches. In this case, reducing the length of the branches may cause the tree either to produce new buds (called adventitious buds) or activate dormant (pre-existing) buds at various positions along the branch. This process of branch length reduction can be carried out on many species simply by cutting back to the desired length during the dormant period. This process is carried out using branch pruners.

3. Refining the image

Once a satisfactory branch structure and budding have been achieved, the new shoots are regularly pinched back. This keeps the growth 'tight', maintains the shape and builds up a very twiggy appearance - the ramification that is so important to the convincing overall tree-like image of the Bonsai. Fingertips are used to pinch out new growth as it is soft and easily removed; scissors take care of older, woody growth.

In addition, there is a technique called 'leaf pruning'. This consists of cutting off all the leaves on a deciduous Bonsai (one that is in good health) after the leaves have emerged and hardened in late spring or early summer. This spurs the tree into producing a fresh crop of leaves which are much smaller. This technique, if regularly carried out, will result in permanently smaller leaves. Some species such as sycamore and trident maple can be leaf-pruned every one or two years quite successfully. However, this process is potentially harmful to the tree and, in reality, the benefits in leaf-size reduction are outweighed by the risk of killing the tree in the process.

Pinching out the soft new growth is the prime technique used in maintaining the shape and size of a Bonsai. It also refines the branch structure and builds a detailed ramification. Although the foliage texture differs in species such as pines (which produce candles) and junipers (scale foliage), the pinching out of unwanted new growth using the fingers is carried out in the same way.

Applying effective Bonsai techniques may reduce leaf size dramatically. On the left a leaf from a sycamore tree growing in the wild; on the right one from a sycamore grown as a Bonsai for over 20 years. The reduction in size is colossal - from 8.5 in. (21.5 cm.) down to 1 in. (2.5 cm.).

Section 1 The craft of Bonsai

Creating driftwood effects

The creation of dead wood areas on Bonsai can have a very dramatic visual effect. Dead wood can enhance the appearance of age, and create an atmosphere of realism. This dead wood is called 'jin' (a Japanese word); the process of creating dead wood is called 'jinning'. This technique is normally carried out on evergreen trees which, although they are called 'softwoods', have wood that is much more resistant to decay and rot than the deciduous 'hardwoods'.

The aim, with these areas of dead wood, is to achieve a lightning-struck appearance, or an appearance of great age as seen on ancient junipers and pines growing naturally in the mountainous regions of the world.

The techniques of creating dead wood and jins are demonstrated in Project 7.

A note of caution: it is currently very fashionable to turn unwanted branches into jins when designing a Bonsai, but this can be overdone. If, for example, a driftwood-style Bonsai is being created with lots of twisted dead-wood areas and a minimum of foliage to reflect its struggle in a mountainous region, then dead wood looks great. However, on a simple Bonsai representing a more placid history, a single branch of white dead wood is distracting and looks out of place. Normally dead wood should be used as the focal point of a Bonsai or not at all.

On large Bonsai, power tools are sometimes used to sculpt the dead wood areas into dramatic shapes. The advent of small electrical hobby drills has enabled many enthusiasts to create living sculptures of their Bonsai.

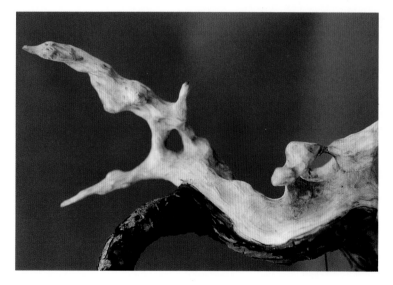

The bleached dead-wood area of a Bonsai. After many hours of patient work an artificially created but intrinsically pleasing shape and texture have been achieved.

Materials for creating Bonsai

Bonsai requires specific materials. This chapter explains these materials and assesses the merits of various plant-material sources. The materials and tools required are now widely available with minimal financial outlay.

The Bonsai grower needs five forms of material: the living plants, tools, pots, soil, and consumables (such as wire).

Sources of tree material

While some species are preferable, with a few exceptions most trees and shrubs can be used for Bonsai. Shrubs differ from trees in that their natural growth habit is to have multiple stems growing from ground level. So far as Bonsai is concerned, the difference therefore is a question of shape definition only. A shrub that is pruned to a single stem can be considered a tree for the purposes of Bonsai.

Plant material suitable for Bonsai can be obtained from any of three sources: it may be self-grown, purchased or collected.

Self-grown Bonsai material includes seeds, cuttings and air-layered plants, in fact anything which entails propagation. Purchased material is the commonest source - there is a multiplicity of garden centres, tree and shrub nurseries, and specialist suppliers open to the public. Collected material from the wild or a garden usually provides the best-quality material, but is sometimes difficult to find.

Each of these methods will now be examined in more detail.

Self-grown material

Sources

Most trees and shrubs can be propagated from seed or cuttings, or by air-layering or grafting. The many methods are described in detail in any gardening book on propagation. Planting out seedlings and cuttings in garden beds will bulk them up much faster than growing them in pots, as there is no restriction of the space available for the root system. This method can be successful, but it may still be years before the trunk has grown sufficiently in girth.

Advantages

Inexpensive.
Air-layering existing branches from trees and shrubs can provide interesting material.
Very large 'cuttings' can be taken from some species. Willow cuttings, for example, will root within weeks if placed in water at any time from spring to late summer. I have seen huge (12 in., 30 cm. girth) willow cuttings propagated this way.

Disadvantages

Very slow. It may takes many years for a seedling or cutting to gain sufficient bulk to be used for Bonsai.

Requires knowledge of the techniques, and skills of propagation.

Tends to engender a sense of 'twig in a Bonsai pot'. Simply potting-up a seedling into a Bonsai pot does not transform it into a Bonsai.

Air-layering of existing trees and shrubs can produce interesting Bonsai material in a short space of time. Here, a collected birch is being air-layered; a section of bark has been removed and moss placed on the area, held in place with polythene wrapped around and secured. The moss is kept moist and in a few months the wounded area will produce roots. It is then separated from the mother plant and planted in a pot. This birch will make a handsome raft-style Bonsai.

30

Summary

Growing one's own material for Bonsai can be very satisfying. However, there is a temptation to start training the material before it is ready.

Purchasing Bonsai material

Sources

Stock plants from garden centres and nurseries are, for the majority of Bonsai enthusiasts, the source of raw plant material, and this is probably the best method for the beginner. The 'reject' or 'bargain' sections of these outlets should also be searched; often material with twisted and deformed trunks or stunted growth can be found. These plants are unsuitable for general sale, but are often just what the Bonsai grower is seeking. Most of the Projects in this book involve the use of purchased material.

Advantages

Readily available from the many outlets selling garden trees and shrubs.

The initial period of bulking up has already passed.

Vast selection to choose from.

Convenience allied with the fun of searching for that special find.

May already have an established, quite fibrous root system.

The modern garden centre - clean, tidy, attractively laid out and convenient with a wide selection of healthy plants - an excellent source of tree and shrub material for the aspiring Bonsai grower.

Nurseries offer the opportunity of rummaging around and discovering something special. This maple has good rootage, a tapering trunk and multiple branches; the emerging red leaves contrast well with its dark-coloured bark - a good choice for Project 1.

Disadvantages
Few. Larger material can sometimes be expensive.

Summary
This is the preferred method of obtaining the raw material to style and train into Bonsai at the outset. As this is such a good source of Bonsai plant material we will look at how a stock plant is selected.

Ten tips for selecting stock plants

1   Check for a good root buttress. This is sometimes below the soil level if the plant has recently been repotted. If this is the case then obtain permission, if possible, to feel down a few centimetres below the soil level to make sure that the desired rootage is present.

2   Ensure the plant is not pot-bound.

3   Choose plants with tapering trunks and interesting bark textures.

4   Excess branches allow for more design options, so the more the better.

5 Choose only healthy plants.

6 Avoid material with branches that lack inner growth, particularly on evergreens, as the Bonsai process invariably requires the shortening of branches. Avoid species with upward dominant (fastigiate) branch growth.

7 Try to visualize generally what shape the final Bonsai would take.

8 If the species is unknown to you ask about its horticultural needs.

9 Check out the 'bargain' and 'reject' sections.

10 Get to know your nurseryman and ask around. Many tips on other sources of material come from the most unexpected people.

Collecting from the wild

Nature is a superb sculptor and there is a wealth of material waiting to be collected and trained into Bonsai. The majority of classic Bonsai have been crafted from material originally collected from the wild.

There are many types of sites where Bonsai material may be located and removed, such as hedges and gardens, woods and forests (particularly horse-riding trails), canals and river-banks, heathland, disused quarries, mountainous areas, construction sites such as road-building construction areas, and farmland.

Note that in the UK, and many other countries, it is **illegal** to remove plants from the wild without first having obtained the permission of the landowner.

Advantages
Wonderful diversity of species and shapes.
Great fun, and very rewarding.
Apart from any travelling costs this material is free.
High quality and available from no other source.
Visiting the countryside gives you the chance to look to examples of mature trees for inspiration.

Disadvantages
Time-consuming.
Can be frustrating if you come back empty-handed.
Difficult to get some species to survive being transplanted.
Permission to collect needs to be obtained.
After collection there can be a long wait before the tree has recovered its health sufficiently to be styled.
Can be VERY hard work.

This small oak has been stunted by the continual attentions of browsing sheep: excellent natural Bonsai material waiting to be collected by an enthusiast.

Summary

The preferred method of obtaining material for the advanced Bonsai grower. Over the years one builds up a stock of raw material, re-establishing itself and waiting to be trained, which makes all the hard work worthwhile.

Tools

Many Bonsai books show a vast array of available tools; this can be daunting for the novice who may feel that a small fortune needs to be spent. In fact, an amateur artist may need only two or three different brushes with which to paint a picture, although a professional artist may have hundreds of different brushes. It is the same with Bonsai - the amateur enthusiast requires only a basic set of tools to start with. As one's experience and commitment to Bonsai grows, so do the number and variety of tools in one's armoury.

Basic Bonsai tools

Sharp, sturdy, clean scissors: either household scissors or garden pruning shears may be used if they meet these criteria.

Pliers: they have many uses and are indispensable. A pair of orthodox workman's or DIY pliers is quite adequate; even better with built-in wire-cutters.

Wire-cutters: the pliers will suffice for most operations; however wire is best removed from the tree by cutting it and then wire-cutters of some description are needed. Electrical wire-cutters are suitable.

Branch-pruners: this specialist Bonsai tool for branches leaves a concave cut; the resulting slight indentation ensures that a clean, flat callous develops with no ugly swelling. Branch-pruners are an invaluable tool for Bonsai.

Root rake: this is used to rake out the roots before cutting them when root-pruning. A strong household fork with the prongs bent over is a cheap and convenient substitute.

Chopstick: this, or a similar blunt tool, is used to settle the soil after re-potting.

Pots

A Bonsai needs to be planted in a container. As a shallow, flat root system enhances the appearance of Bonsai, a shallow, flat pot is normally chosen (except in the case of the cascade style where taller pots are used). Many outlets sell ceramic Bonsai pots, as well as some plastic and mica Bonsai pots which look much the same but provide an inexpensive alternative. Seed trays or any similar-shaped container may be used for Bonsai in training, but once the tree is looking its finest it really deserves an appropriate Bonsai pot. A pot that is too small, large or ugly can spoil the overall impression.

Bonsai pots are produced in a multiplicity of sizes, colours, shapes and materials. Some are glazed with bright colours, others are unglazed with subdued grey and brown finishes. Any pot to be left outside during the winter must be frost-proof. Of course, personal preference plays an important part in Bonsai pot selection - one person's ideal pot is another's nightmare. Above all, choose something that meets the horticultural need for good drainage: after that it really is a personal choice.

A Bonsai tree planted in a round pot is normally positioned in the centre. In a square or rectangular pot it is always planted slightly further back and slightly offset from the centre. This creates asymmetry in the same way as a Bonsai tree itself should be asymmetrical (see page 23).

Soil

The roots of a plant provide it with nutrients, water and anchorage. Two different forms of root exist on all trees - thick tap roots that penetrate deeply and provide a firm foothold, and small fibrous feeder roots with tiny root hairs that absorb water and nutrients through their cell walls by osmosis.

A Bonsai grows in a small pot with limited space for the root system. Tap roots are not required because the tree is anchored firmly in its pot by other means such as wire. It is therefore desirable to minimize the number and size of the thick, redundant tap roots and so allow the smaller feeder roots full rein to use the available growing space. A fibrous root system is what the Bonsai grower is aiming for.

In nature, a tree has a degree of control over the direction its roots grow and can, therefore, adjust somewhat to the environmental conditions at soil level. The roots of a Bonsai have no choice as to their environmental conditions, so special attention must be given to using the correct soil medium.

Ideally a Bonsai soil must have the following attributes:

It must retain moisture.
It must have an open, porous consistency. This provides good drainage which prevents root rot, and allows the passage of air into the minute soil spaces (healthy roots require a small amount of oxygen).

The basic Bonsai soil is a well-mixed combination of 40 per cent grit, 60 per cent proprietary compost, and a little granular fertilizer.

It must not be compacted. Compaction is usually caused by pressing down the soil during re-potting, and destroys the open consistency.

It must be pest- and disease-free. Proprietary composts and grits sold through gardening outlets are used as these will have been sterilized.

It must contain nutrients (see Fertilizer, page 125).

It must have an appropriate level of acidity. Certain species such as azaleas are lime-haters, or calcifuge, and require a relatively acidic soil, in which case an ericaceous compost is used.

These are the requirements. It sounds complicated - but it isn't! A suitable soil mix requires a minimum of effort. A basic soil of approximately 40 per cent grit and 60 per cent proprietary compost, well mixed, will meet the needs of most Bonsai. There is a wide choice of peat-based and peat-free composts, and almost any that is labelled 'multi-purpose' is suitable for the compost component of Bonsai soil. Grit should be a mix of irregular and rounded particles from 2 to 5 mm in size: some potting grit, crushed granite and clean aquarium grits meet this criterion. Large-particle grits (such as gravel) or small-grained sands should not be used.

Consumables

Wire is the main consumable in Bonsai. It is sold by weight (and in metric gauges), so for a given cost one gets a far greater length of thin wire than of a thicker-gauge wire. Bonsai wire is indispensable. It is available from all Bonsai nurseries and suppliers. Buying in bulk rolls of half a kilo or a kilo is cost-effective, but involves a larger initial outlay. When beginning Bonsai, a selection of 250 gm. rolls, one each of 1 mm., 2 mm., 3 mm. and 4 mm., is quite sufficient.

Wound sealant (also called cut paste) is applied to the pruning cuts made on a Bonsai. It generally contains a fungicide which, applied over time, prevents any fungus entering the wound, and helps keep the area moist and so assist the healing process.

Lime sulphur is a chemical which bleaches and preserves dead wood (see Project 7°). It is available from Bonsai nurseries and suppliers.

Mesh is required to cover the large drainage holes in Bonsai pots and so prevent the soil from falling out. This mesh is made of plastic and is sold at garden centre outlets for use as greenhouse shading. See the photographs in the Projects section for examples.

Bonsai equipment summary

The basic set of equipment for Bonsai is quite small. There are no items which are completely indispensable, and many substitutes may be used with ingenuity. With very basic tools and equipment excellent Bonsai can be created. The key to good Bonsai is not the amount spent on a lavish toolkit but rather the appreciation of design, and the after-care needed to maintain them in good health.

36

The basic toolkit of the Bonsai grower.

Ten everyday mistakes

Knowing what not to do is often as helpful as knowing what to do. The following hints are based upon the author's observations on many thousands of Bonsai created by many different people. Some common mistakes are seen time and time again. So, by way of a summary of the first section of this book, and as a preliminary to the Projects in the next section, listed here are ten common mistakes to avoid.

1   Seedlings in Bonsai pots going under the guise of Bonsai.
2   Two-dimensional Bonsai with no back branches.
3   Lack of strong rootage and good taper to the trunk.
4   Over-fertilizing and/or under-watering.
5   Flat tops to the apex that look like a well-clipped hedge, or very pointed triangular tops that make the tree look young and immature.
6   Wiring applied but not securely anchored.
7   Inappropriate and distracting dead-wood jins.
8   Lack of pruning so that the foliage 'closes in' and the Bonsai starts to resemble a dwarf conifer.
9   Attempting to subjugate a poorly chosen species (such as *Leylandii*) into Bonsai.
10 Keeping Bonsai inside the home for extended periods.

One of the author's first attempts at Bonsai fifteen years ago - it demonstrates nearly all the possible mistakes. This is a shabby seedling planted on a monotonous lump of rock - it is not, and probably never will be, a Bonsai.

These mistakes can all be avoided by following the basic principles outlined in the previous chapters, and by carefully following the sequences of Bonsai creation in the next section.

2

The Projects

Preparatory information

The eight projects in this book have all been devised so as to simplify Bonsai technique through pictorial example. Although, at a casual glance, some aspects of the projects may appear difficult in places, it should be possible to carry them through by studying the photographs and reading the accompanying text. The text and photographs provide a comprehensive tutorial for each of the projects. The author has tried to forget his own experience, cast his mind back many years to when he was starting out, and consider the questions he asked and the problems he encountered.

Each project creates a different style of Bonsai; so that, taken together. they make up a small but high-quality, starter Bonsai collection. They have been chosen to demonstrate the various essential elements of design, horticultural and Bonsai shaping techniques, so that an extensive Bonsai 'apprenticeship' may be achieved by tackling all the projects.

Please study the whole project before embarking upon it.

At the start of each project, there is a full-page photograph of the completed Bonsai. The red rules to the right of these photographs indicate the height of the trees: each rule represents 3 in. (7.6 cm.).

Styles of Bonsai

A different style of Bonsai (see page 15) is created in each of the eight projects. As there are more styles than projects it is not possible to cover them all.

Time required

Each project has been designed to be completed in under a day. Some are shorter than others and may be accomplished in a few hours. Everyone works at a different pace so it is not possible to be exact about the time required for each. Rather, it is better to work at one's own pace and take a break now and then.

Difficulty

The projects are arranged in a conscious order so as to teach the techniques of Bonsai in turn: for example the first project demonstrates root-pruning in detail. Other projects use this technique but it is not shown again in such detail.
In general, the projects do not increase in difficulty, although the final project is more challenging than any of the previous ones and does require experience gained from some of them.

Costs

It is impossible to quote costs for the projects, as they are dependent on where and when the projects are being undertaken, and the specific materials you buy (the type of pot chosen can drastically alter the cost: for example a simple temporary plastic pot will cost very little, but a hand-made, high-quality Bonsai pot may be expensive). However, the total cost of each project is estimated at between ten and forty per cent of the cost of purchasing the completed Bonsai from a specialist supplier.

Pots

Various types of pots are used, but in the main this is, again, to illustrate the various types of pot available. If you do not have access to similar pots then this is of no great consequence. Alternatives are mentioned in each of the projects. However, a 'finished' Bonsai does look better in a good pot. In all the projects a temporary container may be used for the first couple of years while a suitable permanent pot is sought out. Specialist Bonsai suppliers carry a range of Bonsai pots and many garden centres now carry a good range of inexpensive Chinese ceramic pots that are suitable.

Root-pruning and repotting

There are two methods of coordinating the root-pruning and repotting of newly-created Bonsai: root-pruning and repotting may be performed at the same time, or one before the other with an interval between (from several days up to several months). Each has its merits. The methods shown within the projects have been chosen to demonstrate the options and to simplify the process. If one is new to Bonsai and the process of root pruning illustrated in the projects looks a little drastic, then do not despair ... all of the featured trees in the projects are healthy a year after the projects were undertaken.

'Materials'

Specific material requirements are outlined in the individual project text.

The number and variety of tools used have been kept to a minimum. Branch-cutters are used in several of the projects. An alternative is to use a sturdy pair of garden pruning shears. Bonsai wire is used in many of them - this is available from all Bonsai nurseries; alternatively, copper electrical wire may be used.
A variety of different soil mixes is shown in the project photographs to demonstrate the various options. In practice the soil mix outlined on pages 34–35 is quite sufficient for the projects.

'Suitable Species'

A variety of species has been chosen for the projects. Overall they represent a cross-section of those available including deciduous, evergreen and flowering species. All are practicable for the Bonsai novice - any special cultural or technical considerations are outlined in the text. The trees and shrubs used have all been bought at little cost from garden centre and nursery outlets. They have been chosen for their availability, resilience and value for money. No special pilgrimages have been made to seek out that extra special material - this would have defeated the purpose. With a minimum of searching they should all be found within your locality. However, suitable substitutes are proposed within the text should any of the species prove difficult to track down in a particular region.

'Season'

Each project contains recommendations for the best time of year to undertake it.
In practice your choice of projects may be restricted due to the time of year.
The projects do not have to be undertaken in the order in which they are set out, provided that the previous ones are studied beforehand to give familiarity with the techniques demonstrated.

'Comments'

The key techniques being demonstrated are indicated here, as well as other useful information. Please read them.

'Aftercare'

Aftercare information and recommendations are given. If any concerns, or unexpected problems occur, then the best advice I can offer is to ask yourself, 'What is best for the tree?', and then to take appropriate measures.

'The future'

After the basic structure of the Bonsai has been achieved, the Bonsai enthusiast needs to decide on the areas of focus for future refinement of the tree. Suggestions on these focus areas are included. Further ideas on refinement may be stimulated by looking at trees in the wild, studying the photographs of completed Bonsai in this book, and visiting Bonsai displays and shows.

A final few words before you embark on the projects: Bonsai is an art form and no artistic skill can be taught completely within the pages of one volume. The projects are intended to demonstrate the techniques in detail, so that the aspiring Bonsai-grower may at least understand the steps necessary to create Bonsai trees. Be bold with the shaping of Bonsai and practise the techniques. The more one practises shaping Bonsai the better the results tend to be. Or, in the words of Mark Twain, 'Experience really is the best teacher. A man who picks up a cat by its tail will probably not make the same mistake a second time.'

If your first attempt at shaping a Bonsai is not completely successful the effort will not have been wasted; the experience will have furthered your skills and will be drawn upon at the next attempt. In time, almost all mistakes may be rectified.

Projects overview

Project	Material	Bonsai style	Key techniques
1	maple	informal upright	root-pruning; potting into a Bonsai container; pruning; branch shortening
2	willow	weeping	wiring (1); pots with single drainage hole
3	beech	group	visual perspective (1) planting onto a slab; applying moss
4	cotoneaster	landscape planting	attachment of Bonsai to rocks; accent plantings; display in a water basin
5	cedar	cascade	potting into a tall pot; re-positioning thick branch; visual perspective (2); pruning - reducing the number of branches
6	azalea	literati	using flowering species; removal of secondary trunk; bending brittle branches; maintenance of lime-hating plants; wiring (2)
7	juniper	slanting windswept	naturalistic planting creation of dead wood - jin and shari; maintenance of dead wood areas
8	Scots pine	triple trunk	use of large material; advanced design considerations; refinement of pine species

Informal upright maple

An informal upright style Bonsai of the maple species reminiscent of a lone tree in the countryside

Materials: single-trunk maple 12-24 in. (30-60 cm.) tall

round, shallow pot	Bonsai wire	basic tools
cut sealant	Bonsai soil	plastic mesh

Suitable species: any of the many varieties of Japanese Maple (*Acer palmatum*). The tree featured here is *Acer palmatum* 'Red Pygmy'. It is worth the effort to find a suitable maple for this project as the foliage is especially attractive, in particular that of the crimsoned-leaved varieties, such as 'Seigen' or 'Deshojo'.

Season: spring is the best time for this project, when the new buds are swelling prior to opening. The tree is preparing to release its stored energy reserve into the new year's growth of leaves and roots. This reawakening process and the inherent vigour of the tree will help it recover from the shock of the Bonsai process. The project could be undertaken at any time from autumn leaf-fall through to late spring, provided frost-free conditions are ensured throughout the winter. The tree featured in the project photographs was styled during late spring when the leaves were just beginning to open, a little later than the ideal time.

Comments: this first project shows the basic techniques of creating a Bonsai from purchased material - the root-pruning and potting of the tree, removal of excess and overly thick branches, and initial wiring.

1 The project materials

This tree was purchased from a garden centre. It is approximately six years old and has already developed some taper to the trunk and the basis of a branch structure. The Bonsai container chosen is slightly larger than that which will be finally used, at the next repotting, so that the tree may be potted with the minimum of root reduction, a safety factor if this is a first attempt at creating a Bonsai. A round container has been chosen as all Bonsai have a front and back, and your first efforts at planting a Bonsai may result in its not being planted in the correct position; using a round pot, it is a simple operation to turn the container to show the correct front view of the tree - a useful tip. Alternatively, any shallow flat container may be used, such as a rigid seed-tray. Other materials required are soil, wire, mesh to cover the drainage holes in the pot, wound sealant and a basic set of tools including a chopstick (or other blunt instrument), root rake, branch cutters, scissors and pliers.

2 Inspecting the material

Many maple varieties are propagated by grafting onto standard *Acer palmatum* root stock. As in this example, select only material where the graft is unobtrusive. Any material with excess swelling at this graft union should be rejected as it is unsightly and will only look worse as the tree ages. The featured tree is 40 cm. (16 in.) tall, an ideal height for a first Bonsai creation - larger may be less manageable and much smaller may be too fiddly.

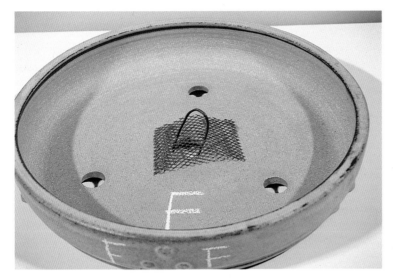

3 Preparing the pot (1)

The preparatory work on the pot is carried out before working on the tree, as this will reduce the time the roots are exposed after they have been pruned. The pot has been examined and the best viewing angle chosen. As with Bonsai trees, pots have a best 'front', particularly if, as in this case, they are handmade. The chosen front to the pot has been marked with chalk as a reminder. A loop of Bonsai wire is passed through a piece of plastic mesh used to cover the drainage hole to prevent the soil from falling out. Good drainage is very important, so pots with large drainage holes are always preferred.

4 Preparing the pot (2)

The ends of the wire, which have been passed through the drainage hole, are bent flat underneath the pot, securing the mesh in place to stop it sliding away when soil is added.

5 Preparing the pot (3)

Mesh is applied to the drainage holes until they are all covered. A long loop of wire is pushed down through one of the drainage holes and up through another on the opposite side of the pot. This wire will be tightened over the top of the rootball to hold the tree securely in the pot. This is important as there will be a tendency for the newly potted tree to rock when first planted. Holding it securely ensures that the delicate new roots that grow are not damaged by any movement of the tree.

Project 1   Informal upright maple

6 Root-pruning (1)

The maple is removed from the container by firmly grasping the base of the trunk and turning the pot upside-down, then applying a sharp tap to the base of the pot. This will loosen the soil around the edge of the pot and free the rootball. A shaded position is best for the root-pruning process as this helps prevent sun and wind drying the exposed roots.

An alternative approach, although it prolongs the creation process, is to prune the roots after the tree has been restyled: this has certain advantages, in that full soil reserves are available for the plant's recovery after restyling, the relationship between removed roots and removed branches becomes less critical, and the selection of the pot may be aesthetically more straightforward after the restyled Bonsai can be seen in its new form.

7 Root-pruning (2)

The soil is raked away starting from the edges of the rootball and progressing inwards. In this example, as the tree has been planted in the container less than a year ago, the roots have not filled the capacity of the pot. Should they have done so then a more vigorous approach to root-pruning is indicated.

8 Root-pruning (3)

Removal of soil continues, with special attention to exposing the base of the trunk. The root buttress, which was below the level of the soil, is now exposed. When potted this is one of the elements that will contribute to the overall effect of the tree now assuming a Bonsai shape.

9 Root-pruning (4)

The root-pruning is nearly complete, but there is an unsightly root growing upwards.

10 Root-pruning (5)

This root is removed using the branch-cutters. Scissors could be used, but the branch-cutters are more sturdy and ensure a clean cut is made. As the root was thin no wound sealant was applied to the cut end, but on a thick root this would need to be done (to slow down or prevent the dessication of adjacent tissue, and to reduce fungus attack through the open wound).

11 Root-pruning (6)

If the process of root-pruning is taking some time, then mist the roots lightly to prevent them drying out. The root system has only been pruned lightly - best if you are new to Bonsai. The root-pruned tree is offered up to the pot to ensure the rootball will fit comfortably. If it is too large then it is further root-pruned. (Once one's skills and confidence have grown the rootball can be pruned more drastically in a project such as this.) The remaining soil medium in which the tree was growing is also left untouched - it is quite adequate for the time being. In future years at each repotting, a portion of this 'old' soil will be removed.

Project 1   Informal upright maple

12 Potting-up (1)

A thin layer of Bonsai soil is placed into the base of the pot. The mesh used to cover the drainage holes stops the soil from falling through.

13 Potting-up (2)

The tree is placed in the pot with the best viewing angle of the root buttress and trunk shape facing the front of the pot; the ends of the fixing wire are pulled up and bent over the top of the rootball. In a round pot one can simply position the tree in the middle. If a rectangular pot is used the Bonsai should always be placed slightly further back and to one side, creating additional visual perspective.

14 Potting-up (3)

The ends of the fixing wire are twisted together and tightened firmly with the pliers. The tree is now secured into the pot and will not rock around. This fixing wire can be removed at a later date once the tree has generated new roots and is stable.

15 Potting-up (4)

Additional soil is added and distributed using a blunt chopstick or similar implement. The chopstick is placed in the soil and 'waggled'. This helps the soil settle slightly and ensures no large air pockets remain. Nothing sharp should be used for this process as it may puncture and damage the roots.

16 Never compress Bonsai soil!

This is the wrong method. Never be tempted to compress the soil to provide extra stability for the tree. The tiny air spaces between the soil particles are important for the horticultural health of the roots. Compressing the soil removes these small air spaces and will eventually cause the soil to turn sour.

17 Refining the branches (1)

The overall shape of the finished Bonsai is determined by the initial make-up of the branch system. In this case the tree already has the natural appearance of a spreading, rounded tree as seen in open countryside, so this will be the final image as well. The shaping process now involves removing thick upper branches and wiring a few of the branches so they may be placed in positions where there is a large gap in the current branch structure.

In a healthy young plant such as this, new shoots will grow thick and fast. There are many large, thick branches which make the tree look top-heavy. These branches are reduced in length, always cutting back to a smaller twig. If there is no smaller twig further down the branch then just reduce the branch and wait: new buds and shoots will soon sprout. The branch can then be cut further back to these new twigs.

51

Project 1   Informal upright maple

18 Refining the branches (2)

This thick branch is cut cleanly at its base using the branch cutters. The cut is made at a slant to ensure that water will not collect on the cut end and cause rotting. If branch-cutters are not available a sharp pair of scissors could be used. The smaller twigs growing around its base form the new branches.

19 Refining the branches (3)

The cut is covered with wound sealant. This will keep the cut clean and disease-free and ensure it will heal over cleanly.

The process of removing the overly thick branches continues.

20 Wiring the branches

Wiring of branches is the final process required to finish this Bonsai. In this example only a few are wired to new positions to fill in gaps where there is a lack of branches. These branches will form the framework on which the twiggy sub-branches will be built up over the next few years. It is always best to use a single piece of Bonsai wire to shape two branches: in this way each acts as an anchor for the wire. This is the basic and most important wiring technique.

21 The completed Bonsai

With some basic techniques, a Bonsai has been created in just a few hours. Although still in its infancy as a Bonsai, it already has the required elements of a tree found in nature - a solid root buttress, a tapering trunk, multiple branches and a rounded apex.

If your first attempt bears little resemblance to the one featured here, don't despair! The important thing is that the Bonsai should appeal to your own eyes. One of the joys of the hobby is the opportunity to retrain Bonsai many times during their lives. They continually grow so there will be ample opportunity to correct any mistakes and further improve the shape in years to come. At this stage do not be tempted to keep working on the tree; it is better horticultural practice to allow a recovery period during the summer.

Final height of the Bonsai including pot is 20 in.(51 cm.).

Aftercare

After thoroughly watering the soil and leaving it to drain, the Bonsai is placed in an airy, but frost-free environment. Soon the leaves will emerge and new roots will establish themselves. Only light pinching of the new shoots will be performed during the summer as the tree needs a period of sustained growth to recover from the shock of the Bonsai process. Maples are very prone to leaf scorch during the height of summer, so some light shading should be provided.

The future

Next spring any over-long new shoots will be shortened before the leaves emerge. The main efforts of the Bonsai grower are now directed to building up a very twiggy canopy. This is achieved by allowing growth of new shoots, then reducing their length at the end of the summer. Applying only low doses of fertilizer and slightly reducing the watering will restrict the gaps between the leaves of the new shoots. The Bonsai will be removed from its pot two years after the styling exercise and the roots inspected. If there is still room for growth within the existing container then it will not be root-pruned and repotted until the following year (three years after the styling).

Project 2 Weeping willow

A weeping-style willow Bonsai replicating a mature
riverside willow whose branches cascade downwards

Materials: young willow tree   soil   tall pot
                mesh   Bonsai wire   wound sealant
                basic tools

Suitable species: almost any member of the willow family that develops long
shoots. Weeping Willow (*Salix babylonica*), commonly available, is the most
obvious choice. In the featured project, the Scarlet Willow (*Salix alba
britzensis*) has been used for its attractive orange/red branches. The tamarisk
(*Tamarix* ssp.) could also be used.

Season: spring to mid-summer is the optimum, although any time of year
is suitable.

Comments: This is an ideal beginners' project - it requires few materials and
minimum experience. It focuses on wiring - willow are excellent for
practising this technique as their branches are supple and forgiving of
inexperienced hands. Willow is perhaps the easiest of trees to take cuttings
from, and this technique is demonstrated at the start of the project. Willow
can also be purchased with ease, and the featured project tree was bought to
show an alternative species to the standard weeping willow.

55

Willow cuttings

1 Willow cuttings (1)

Any size of branch may be used as a willow cutting. A particularly interesting branch can be severed to form an attractive trunk to the Bonsai. In this case a few different branches were cut whilst on a walk in the countryside during the spring.

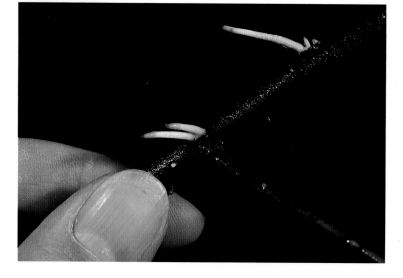

3 Willow cuttings (3)

In just three weeks the immersed areas of the branches are sending out new roots. They will be left in the water for several more weeks until the new roots are more fully developed. Then they are potted up into large flower-pots with care taken not to damage the delicate new roots: a very fast and easy way of obtaining raw material at almost no cost.

2 Willow cuttings (2)

The branches are shortened if necessary and placed in a tub of water where they will quickly issue new roots. No special preparations are needed. The tub of 'cuttings' is left in an airy, partially shaded position and the water topped up when necessary.

Willow Project

4 **The project materials**

A scarlet willow has been used as this has the bonus of attractive branch colour in the winter. Basic tools, soil, mesh, wound sealant and Bonsai wire (2 mm. gauge) are required. Being trees of the waterside, willow consume copious amounts of water and their root systems grow quickly; therefore a deep pot is used which acts as a bigger reservoir for holding moisture and provides a large volume for the roots to grow into.

5 **Preparing the pot**

In the previous project a fixing wire was threaded through two drainage holes and twisted over the rootball to hold the newly potted tree in position. In this project securing the tree is slightly more complex as the container has only one drainage hole. A piece of wire is twisted round a rigid piece of wood or wire and the two ends pushed up through the drainage hole. The rootball will now be secured in the normal way.

6 **Root pruning**

The rootball is removed from the pot and excess roots raked out and cut as demonstrated in Project 1. An extra bonus of a large pot is that the rootball need be only lightly root-pruned to fit into it.

7 Potting the tree

The tree is positioned in the middle of the pot with the trunk slightly tilting - this will give a more natural appearance to the completed Bonsai. A standard soil mix is added and the fixing wire twisted over the rootball and tightened.

8 Watering (1)

As willow require a lot of water it is customary to stand them permanently in a saucer of water throughout the summer. Normally this is done after the completion of the Bonsai process, but in this case the piece of wood used to hold the fixing wire slightly protrudes from the base of the pot. Placing some grit in the saucer keeps the pot stable while the tree is further shaped.

9 Watering (2)

The tree is now well-watered. After the root-pruning exercise the roots will have dried slightly. As the tree is already in leaf it is imperative that it be given water now.

10 Watering (3)

Water is also poured into the saucer to ensure the tree can absorb as much as it needs.

11 Repotting completed

The newly potted willow is now left in the shade
for a couple of hours to rest before it is wired.

12 Removal of dead wood (1)

Now is the time to refine any old dead branch
stumps by cutting them flush to the trunk using the
branch-cutters.

Project 2   Weeping willow

13 Removal of dead wood (2)

The cut is now sealed with wound sealant. The branch-cutters have ensured a clean concave cut which will heal over and leave no ugly swelling.

14 Wiring the branches (1)

ALL the branches on the tree will be wired. The branches are wired in pairs using a single piece of wire for each two branches.

15 Wiring the branches (2)

The wire has been applied not too tightly and not too loosely. The spirals of wire are evenly spaced. The wire needs to extend to only half the length of each branch as the bends will all be made close to the branches' points of origin.

16 Branch-bending (1)

Branches are bent downwards by placing both hands on a branch and gently but firmly bending and then moving the hands a centimetre along and continuing the bend.

17 Branch-bending (2)

A gentle curve is introduced which does not apply too much force on any single part of the branch and risk breaking it.

18 Branch-bending (3)

The branch direction has been changed through 180 degrees by introducing this graceful bend.

19 Branch-bending (4)

The technique of wiring and bending is continued. Any small, short shoots are removed, particularly from the inner areas, as these are too small to be used in the design and would make the image look cluttered.

20 Branch-bending (5)

The apex of the tree shows the form of the completed branches. Care has been taken that the branches cascade in all directions so that the completed Bonsai is three-dimensional.

21 The completed Bonsai
The Bonsai has been turned and viewed from each direction to find the most pleasing angle. In this case the trunk line and rootage did not indicate a stronger front than any other position, so this Bonsai may be viewed from any side.

Final height of the Bonsai
including pot is 19 in. (48 cm.).

63

Aftercare

The completed Bonsai is placed in a lightly shaded, airy position, kept well-watered and misted frequently. When new growth appears the tree is moved to a better-lit position.

The future

The branches will set in their new positions in just a few weeks. The wire is removed as soon as it appears to be constricting the branches (after just a few weeks in the case of this fast-growing willow). Any new small shoots are removed unless they are needed to fill a 'gap' in the design, in which case they will be allowed to grow longer and then wired.

During the winter all the branches will be cut back hard, and in the following spring the new branches once again wired into the weeping position.

Willow Bonsai are root-pruned annually in the spring.

Project 2   weeping willow

Project 3 Beech tree group

A group planting of beech trees representing a small wood or coppice growing on a hill

Materials: beech saplings   flat slab   scissors

cut sealant   compost   moss

no Bonsai wire required

Suitable species: small beech saplings, or hornbeam, are ideal for this project; they are both commonly available as hedging material. Alternatively larch would be a good choice.

Season: spring, just before the buds open. Beech is one of the last species to come into leaf in the spring. Alternatively any time from autumn to spring provided frost-free aftercare is given.

Comments: this project shows how perspective is achieved by a basic design technique, and also by a little visual trickery. The design technique is to place the smaller trees in the background (as explained on pages 67–68) and the visual trick is to create a small path running through the group which heightens the scale of the trees themselves. In addition the use of moss is demonstrated.

1 The project materials

The trees have come from a nursery. There are two four-year-old (the largest), several two-year-old and a few one-year-old saplings. They have all been lightly root-pruned in preparation, and temporarily 'heeled-in' to pots with some loose compost. Beech (and hornbeam) saplings are grown in open ground and lifted by nurseries in the winter for sale as hedging stock. Many nurseries will allow you to choose the individual plants yourself. It is important to get a mix of different heights, trunk thicknesses and shapes for this Bonsai planting. The total number of trees is not important - anything between ten and twenty. In the example a flat man-made resin slab has been used - it is attractive and lightweight. Alternatively, any flat piece of stone or slate could be used, or a very shallow Bonsai pot or large seed tray. No drainage holes are needed on a slab as the mound of soil is exposed on all sides and will drain freely.

2 Preparing the soil (1)

Standard proprietary compost is used, either peat-based or peat-free; it must have a fibrous content which will help it hold together when moist. Water is mixed into the compost as though one were making pastry. The objective is a moist consistency that will hold together. If too much water is added and the mixture turns to sludge then this is easily rectified by adding more compost.

3 Preparing the soil (2)

Just the right consistency - holding together when squeezed, but still crumbly and friable. Balls of soil are going to be moulded around each of the rootballs so that the trees will be held in position when placed on the slab.

4 Positioning the main trees (1)

This is the position chosen for the two trees. The key to achieving a convincing image of a small forest is to spend time on the main focal trees at the front of the group. These are the two largest; alternatively a single tree or more than two could be used. They are turned every which way to find a harmony between the two trunks and the existing branch structure.

Project 3　Beech tree group

5 Positioning the main trees (2)

Incorrect. In this position the two trunks do not 'gel' together, the curves on the bottom halves of the trunks work against each other visually, and the whole image is less pleasing than the previous one.

6 Positioning the main trees (3)

The two main trees are reduced in size. This is not the final height reduction, but will help in determining the position of the subsidiary trees.

7 Positioning the main trees (4)

Good! The positions have been decided and the trees reduced in height: now to plant them on the slab.

8 Planting the trees (1)

The two main trees are placed in position on the slab at one side - not in the middle. The whole group will be positioned to one side as an asymmetrical arrangement is more attractive and looks less artificial. Moist compost is applied round the roots and moulded round the whole root system.

9 Planting the trees (2)

The main trees in place, already the group is starting to take shape. Now is the time to step back, have a cup of tea or coffee and review the positions of these two trees. If they are not in harmony then re-position them. These main trees are the building blocks of the whole group, so they must be correctly placed.

10 Planting the trees (3)

Four of the medium-sized saplings are positioned close behind the two main trees. It is important to plant the trunks fairly close together but at varying distances apart, not evenly spaced. Some branches and roots may need to be pruned away for the trees to fit closely together. The two main trees are now reduced to their final height. The decision on their height is made much easier now that some of the secondary trees have been added. Cut sealant is applied to the wounds where the trunks have been reduced.

11 Planting the trees (4)

A medium-sized tree with more curves in the trunk is placed on the right-hand side of the planting. This tree will hold together that side of the group visually. More compost is added and patted down in place.

Project 3   Beech tree group

12 Planting the trees (5)

More trees are added, including some of the smallest at the back of the group. The small trees add perspective - they look as though they are in the far distance, when actually they are only a few centimetres behind the main trees. Two other effects combine to add realism - the trunks sometimes appear to touch and obscure each other, and the edges of the group point slightly outwards. The positioning of the trees is now complete; the soil mass holds the group together without the need for wiring the trees to the slab.

13 Rear view

From the back the reasons for the positioning of the main trees at the front are apparent - they are partly obscured by the smaller trees. The perspective from the back just does not look realistic.

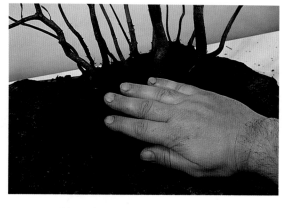

14 Smoothing the soil

This is the one occasion when patting the soil with the hands is permitted. It is lightly patted down, but not too forcefully. Although the soil has lost its open texture, this is only temporary - water is currently occupying the spaces between the soil particles. As the soil dries air will flow in and restore the openness of the texture.

15 Final adjustments

Any small adjustments to the positions of the trees are made and the soil is mounded up and around the whole root system. The roots of the trees will grow together into one inseparable mass, and in future the group will be root-pruned and managed as a single Bonsai.

16 Adding moss (1)

Pieces of moss are planted onto the outside of the root mass. The moss serves two purposes - it binds the whole structure together and acts as a porous 'pot' keeping the soil in place - stopping it from being washed away when the group is watered. The moss stays on permanently and the pieces will grow together and form an attractive natural covering, symbolically representing grass. There are many varieties of moss, but the best is the very low-growing variety found on paving slabs, driveways and paths. Moss from forest locations invariably grows too tall and looks shabby very quickly. The moss used here has been collected from a friend's driveway simply by scraping it up with a blunt knife.

17 Adding moss (2)

The technique for planting the moss is to push the edges into the soil with the fingertips, then press down into the middle of each piece. It will stay in place without any other aids.

18 Adding moss (3)

Moss is placed round the bottom of the root system, but some areas on the top are left bare. This will help with watering and also looks more natural.

Project 3   Beech tree group

19 Creating additional perspective (1)
An area at the front is left free of moss as a path is to be created with small, light-coloured gravel. It will start out wider at the front of the planting, twisting and narrowing towards the back. This visual trick works wonderfully in adding perspective.

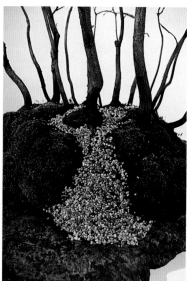

20 Creating additional perspective (2)
The gravel is added and lightly tapped down into the moist soil. One or two small roots at the bases of the trees have been cleaned of soil which also adds to the impression of realism.

21 View from above
Looking down at the group you can see the distribution of the trunks and the branches.

22 The completed group

In a few hours, at minimum cost, and with just a few basic techniques, a convincing image of a small forest has been achieved. Already the young saplings appear to have aged many years. The path has created additional perspective - our eyes see a path and automatically our brain scales up the impression of the height of the trees. The left-hand side of the slab is left unplanted - the area of space also enhances the impression of openness and realism.

The final height of the Bonsai including pot is 23 in. (58 cm.).

73

Aftercare

The whole group is thoroughly watered and placed in an airy location. The leaves will soon emerge and the new shoots will be allowed unrestricted growth for the whole of the summer. This will restore vigour and give the roots an opportunity to grow and bind together so that by the following season the group will be a single entity. Beech are sometimes attacked by white aphids on the undersides of the leaves, so keep a watchful eye. If found they will be wiped away with a damp cloth.

The future

Improving the branch structure will be the main focus for the next few years. By repeated growing and pruning of the shoots a twiggy, well-ramified appearance will develop. The whole group will be treated as an individual Bonsai and root-pruned and replanted onto the slab in two years' time.

Project 3   Beech tree group

Project 4 Landscape planting on rock

A tall rocky outcrop rising from a lake or the sea

Materials: textured piece of rock   selection of small alpines
compost   small stock plant   moss
wire   strong adhesive   basic tools

Suitable species: the key to the success of this landscape is the use of a rock or
stone with a variable and interesting texture. A small stock plant is used as the
main tree with additional alpine plants as accents. A cotoneaster has been used
in the project as this species is widely available and has tiny leaves.

Season: any time of the year.

Comments: this project demonstrates the method of attaching a Bonsai to a piece
of rock. Of all the projects this one most conveys a sense of freedom and
creativity. There is no right or wrong way to position the plants on the rock -
it is a matter of offering them up in different positions until a pleasing and
satisfactory image is achieved.

1 Choosing the rock (1)

Rock and stone is sold through garden centres and stone suppliers. The Bonsai creator must look for a piece of rock with an interesting appearance and texture. Rock quarried by blasting often looks fresh and unnatural and is unsuitable. The rocks here are water-worn limestone which has a lovely, eroded texture. Some rock is very heavy and may not prove practical. If this is the case a smaller rock is chosen, or something lighter in weight such as tufa (a lightweight, porous rock).

The left-hand rock is used for this project. The right-hand rock has been given to one of the author's students to plant up using the project notes and photographs. The two rocks will then be displayed together.

2 Choosing the rock (2)

The selected rock is turned in every direction to find the best position. It must be stable so that it will free-stand and have hollows to act as planting-pockets. If an image of a mountain or island is being sought (as in this case), then the rock looks best 'standing up'. If a hillside scene is wanted then it is better to lay it on its 'side'. The rock is washed to remove any dust and grime and allowed to dry.

3 The project materials

A selection of small plants and alpines is shown: only a few will be used for this actual planting. An adhesive is needed (to attach fixing wires to the rock) - choose one that sets quickly and bonds both stone and metal. A shallow ceramic tray will be used to display the planting when it is finished. The tray here is a strong, purpose-built one without drainage holes. The rock will be placed in it and water added to create a realistic and natural scene of a rocky outcrop rising from an area of water. The water also helps to maintain a high humidity level around the completed planting.

4 Positioning the main tree (1)

This small cotoneaster has been root-pruned and shortened in height. It will be positioned first as it is the main focal point of the planting. It can now be styled by additional pruning and wiring, or (as in this case) this can be delayed until a later date when it has had an opportunity to establish itself on the rock.

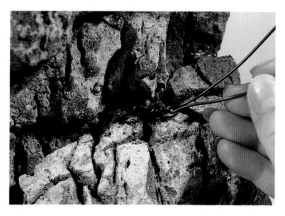

7 Attaching the main tree (1)

The rootball will need to be held firmly in place. Two wires are going to be attached to the rock to secure the tree in position. A piece of wire is twisted at its end and some adhesive pushed into a crevice. The rock must be dry before the adhesive is applied.

5 Positioning the main tree (2)

An alternative position on top of the rock.

6 Positioning the main tree (3)

This is the chosen position. Any of the three positions is suitable, but in this one the tree appears to be clinging tightly to the rock face and looks very natural.

8 Attaching the main tree (2)

The wire is pushed into the adhesive and extra adhesive smeared over the end of the wire. Another wire is also attached by this method a few centimetres to one side. While the adhesive is hardening the rest of the planting can be started.

9 Adding the plants (1)

Compost is moistened (as in Project 3) and pushed into a crevice. An alpine is then planted into the crevice and additional compost smoothed over the rootball. All the other plantings on the rock will be attached using this method. The plants are small and do not need to be wired into place.

10 Adding the plants (2)

Moss is pushed into the compost - this helps hold the plant in position and will stop the soil washing away.

78

11 Adding the plants (3)

A small yellow thyme is planted - this will add a splash of colour to the final planting. A layer of moss is planted running down from the top of the rock to where the main tree is to be positioned. This gives a realistic appearance.

12 Adding the plants (4)

The adhesive has hardened and the main tree is secured by twisting the fixing wires over the rootball. Additional compost is placed over the rootball and moss added. The process of squeezing compost onto the rock and placing moss onto it continues: the goal is to achieve planted sections with areas of rock protruding from them. It is tempting to use all the crevices in the rock as planting pockets for the moss, but some should be left free. An alpine plant has been positioned on the left-hand side - its small size creates perspective as it appears to be further in the distance.

79

13 Adding the plants (5)

More mossy areas are created.

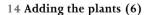

14 Adding the plants (6)
The planting is regularly sprayed to keep it moist.

15 Planting completed
The rock has now been planted with sufficient moss and small plants. If this final appearance is lacking realism it is a simple matter to remove pieces of moss and try them in different positions until a satisfactory image is achieved.

16 Planting completed - side view
The natural protrusions of the rock can be clearly seen.

17 Refining the image
The rock has been placed in the water tray - offset to one side to create an asymmetrical appearance. Another small rock has been placed nearer the front with a small flowering alpine planted on it. Some gravel is laid between the two rocks and water poured into the tray. A few leaves of a pond plant floating on the water surface give a nice final touch.

18 The final planting

The rock from this project and the one created by the author's student are positioned together. The chasm formed at the junction of the two rocks lends credibility and interest to the final image.

Final height of the Bonsai including pot is 14 in. (36 cm.).

Aftercare

The completed Bonsai is placed in a lightly shaded, airy position. It must be watered frequently to prevent the moss from drying out and falling off. A good tip is to ensure the moss extends to the base of the rock and touches the water. It then acts as a wick and draws up water to the whole planting by capillary action. The planting must be kept shaded from summer sun as it may dry out very quickly.

The future

All the elements of the planting will mature. Their roots will grow down into the crevices of the rock and attach themselves permanently. Fertilizer will be given only sparingly: small holes are made in the moss near the plants and a few grains of granular fertilizer put in them; alternatively the planting can be fed with a soluble foliar feed. All the plants will be pruned each year to keep them small. The main tree will be refined over the next couple of years. In three or four years' time the main tree will be root-pruned by scraping away some of the soil and cutting back some of the roots *in situ* without removing it from the rock. Fresh soil will be added and moss placed on top.

Project 4   Landscape planting on rock

Project 5 Cascade-style cedar

An ancient tree growing on a mountainside. Buffeted by wind, damaged by rock-falls and weighed down by snow and ice, it stubbornly clings to the rock face, defying the very elements that have shaped it

Materials: tree or shrub with at least one long low branch

tall Bonsai container	soil	mesh
wound sealant	Bonsai wire	tools
small saw		

Suitable species: the tree is *Cedrus deodara*, a member of the cedar family, chosen because of its short trunk and long, low branches. The cedars have an attractive needle type, very reminiscent of pines. As the style symbolizes trees found at high altitudes the most suitable species are evergreens, particularly pine, juniper or cedar, but it is more important for this style of Bonsai to select a specimen that has the long low branch and short trunk - 'prostrate' varieties often meet these requirements.

Season: apart from high summer, this project can be carried out at any time of the year provided sensible aftercare is given. In winter the completed Bonsai must be kept frost-free; in late spring or autumn shading must be given to prevent sun scorching and dehydration.

Comments: this creation shows the techniques of repositioning a thick branch and removal of large amounts of foliage to expose the hidden form within.

1 The plant material

This tree was bought from a nursery. It is about eight years old. Its excellent health can be judged by its vigour and foliage colour.

2 Branch removal

There are two long, low branches: the shorter is removed. The other will form the main hanging branch of the cascade. At this stage all over-long branches are generally shortened so the tree is easier to work on.

3 Planting angle

It has been placed at the approximate planting angle. The main short trunk tapers nicely up towards the apex.

4 Wiring of main branch (1)

A long piece of Bonsai wire is applied to the entire length of the main branch. It must have sufficient holding power. If the branch is thinner in diameter a smaller-gauge wire should be used, and the converse applies.

5 Wiring of main branch (2)

The branch is wired at this early stage before repotting. This helps one assess the planting angle and it is much easier to apply a long length of wire at this stage.

6 Pot selection

The branch is bent downwards and the overall height compared with the pot. Once repotted, the hanging branch should not touch the ground. If it does, then it is shortened. In this cascade style the pot also acts as a symbolic cliff face; therefore a slightly rugged pot is better than a very smooth, shiny, glazed one. The pot is 33 cm. (13 in.) tall. Alternatively, any tall container may be used - even a plastic flower pot if that is all that is available.

7 Inspection of roots

The plastic pot is removed and the roots inspected. They are healthy and vigorous, so repotting may proceed.

Project 5   Cascade-style cedar

8 Reducing the rootball (1)

The rootball is carefully reduced using a root-rake. As cascade pots are tall with relatively small openings, the rootball will normally have to be drastically reduced, as here.

9 Reducing the rootball (2)

Nearly there. A final trim with sharp, clean scissors and it is ready for repotting. The rootball has been extensively reduced, quite safe if a similar ratio of foliage is also removed. Don't forget to mist the roots if the process of reducing the rootball takes quite a while.

10 Soil drainage layer

The pot is prepared with mesh and wire in the normal manner. A very coarse layer of gravel is put in first. This ensures good drainage, important with such a tall pot. In a shallow Bonsai container this separate drainage layer is not normally needed.

11 Adding soil

The pot is then further filled with a standard, gritty Bonsai soil mix. The root-pruned tree has been held next to the pot to show how much soil should be poured into the pot before the tree goes in. There must be no gap between the rootball and the soil as this would inhibit the growth of new roots.

12 Final root reduction

A few longer roots have been kept at the base of the rootball to encourage downward growth of the new roots.

13 Finishing repotting

Additional soil is added and settled using a blunt chopstick. The wire ends are now placed over the rootball and the wire tightened. The wire holds the tree firmly in place; the temptation to compress the soil with the fingers must be resisted as this will cause compaction.

Project 5   Cascade-style cedar

14 Completion of repotting

The cascade-style Bonsai after repotting. Already the desired image is beginning to take shape. Time for a well-earned break. Now is the time to step back and assess progress so far, and plan the fine tuning of the branches.

15 Lowering of main branch (1)

Side view - and there is a problem! The main hanging branch does not fall at a sufficiently acute angle. It is too thick to allow a sharp bend to be introduced, so an alternative technique must be used to lower it further.

16 Lowering of main branch (2)

The area on the branch where the bend is needed is partly sawn through, in this case at the junction of the branch and trunk. The wire holds the branch firmly while this operation is carried out. There is no danger to the health of the branch as the intact bottom area will maintain the flow of water from the roots and trunk.

17 Lowering of main branch (3)

The cut branch is gently lowered, while listening for any ominous cracking sounds. If it is moved firmly but gently there should be no problems.

18 Lowering of main branch (4)

The gap is now filled with cut sealant. This helps the wound heal quickly by preventing it drying out. The wire will be left on until the cut has completely calloused over. There is a bonus with this technique - when the cut is healed this scarred area will become rigid and hold the hanging branch very firmly in position.

Project 5   Cascade-style cedar

19 Final shaping

More foliage is removed. This style requires a slightly sparse appearance on the hanging branch to prevent it looking unstable. There is no definitive technique for fine tuning of the smaller branches. Make small adjustments then step back to see whether the changes have worked visually; if not then try them in a slightly different position. These small adjustments must be carried out with sensitivity and gentleness; any excess pulling and pushing will result in the bark separating, causing the branch to die.

20 Final touches

Almost complete. All the small branches have been wired and placed at a downward angle to give an overall impression of age, and an image that is credible and satisfying. The small branches appear to 'float', achieved by making many very small adjustments to their positions. There is ample material left for cuttings!

21 Side view of apex

The apex of the completed Bonsai points forward and the back branch is longer than the front ones (the design technique discussed in Visual Perspective, page 22).

22 The completed Bonsai

The completed Bonsai reflects the natural style very well. The glazing marks near the base of the pot echo the image of the branches - a nice touch, not essential but helping convey the atmosphere of a rugged mountainside.

Final height of the Bonsai including pot is 21 in. (53 cm.).

Aftercare

The pot is placed nearly to its rim in a bucket of water and left for no more than a few hours - the soil will absorb water by capillary action (it is a good idea always to water cascade-style Bonsai by this method). It is then placed in a frost-free environment with good air circulation and the foliage misted daily. This helps the tree to form new buds, and absorb water while its root system recovers from root-pruning.

The future

After the rigours of the styling exercise the Bonsai will be allowed full rein to grow and regain its vigour over the next growing season.

Further repotting will not be undertaken for at least three years as there is ample space in the tall pot for the roots to grow and develop, with no risk of them becoming pot-bound. The piece of wire on the main cascading branch will be left in place until the cut at the base has healed over. This will be in about two or three years' time.

The foliage pads will be encouraged to develop, but all emergent shoots that grow directly downwards from the branches are removed to help the 'floating' image. Try to imagine the foliage pads as flowing into one another as water does in a series of waterfalls, and prune them to this shape accordingly.

Project 6 Literati flowering azalea

The literati style of Bonsai most succinctly captures
the Oriental view of nature

Materials: tall tree or shrub - preferably a flowering variety

round pot soil	mesh	tools
wound sealant	Bonsai wire	raffia

Suitable species: the featured azalea is the sort of material often found in the 'bargain' section of a nursery or garden centre. It is quite unattractive and has developed a long trunk with little taper. Almost any species with a long trunk is suitable for this project, and this style is sometimes a good way of making use of material that is too 'leggy' for any other style of Bonsai. Flowering species, particularly members of the azalea and prunus families, make excellent literati Bonsai.

Season: flowering species are normally repotted just after flowering, or sometimes before, so this is the best time of year for the project. However, provided the root reduction is not extreme, the project could be tackled at any other time of year.

Comments: this project demonstrates a method for bending very brittle branches (a feature of azaleas), maintenance of lime-hating plants, removal of secondary trunk and wiring techniques.

1 The materials

The normal materials are required - tools, wire, mesh, wound sealant and soil. This style of Bonsai looks best in a round container. Raffia and a small saw are also needed.

2 Removal of secondary trunk (1)

The tree has been root-pruned and potted in the normal way. The trunk leans slightly to one side in the planting position - this is deliberate, as it induces the flowing feeling of this style. Positioning the trunk pointing straight upwards would be a mistake. The old secondary trunk is dead and needs to be removed. It is sawn through, close to the trunk, and the wound refined using the branch-cutters. If carving implements are available it would be a good idea to shape this area adding additional interest.

3 Removal of secondary trunk (2)

The cut area is now covered with wound sealant - this is most important with the azalea species as they are prone to infection from open wounds.

4 Bending brittle branch (1)

This branch needs to be lowered. It is very brittle and if bent in the normal way will probably snap. To protect it, raffia is moistened and wrapped around the area.

5 Bending brittle branch (2)

The raffia is wound all along the branch. It now forms a surrogate secondary bark and, although flexible, will add strength to the branch when it is bent.

Project 6   Literati flowering azalea

6 Bending brittle branch (3)

The branch is wired and gently bent to the required position.

7 Wiring of branches (1)

All the branches and twigs will be wired and positioned. The branch positioned using the raffia will be wired first of all.

8 Wiring of branches (2)

Every twig is wired (using 1 and 2 mm gauge wire) and then positioned to create a spade-shaped foliage area when viewed from above.

9 Removal of excess branches

The two top left-hand branches are removed (one of them in this example was wired by mistake!) to leave three branches only. The decision to remove them is based on two factors: they are both too long, and together with the remaining branches would make the final Bonsai look top-heavy.

10 Wiring of branches (3)

The two remaining branches are wired and positioned.

Project 6   Literati flowering azalea

11 Wiring of branches (4)

The twigs are all wired and positioned in the same manner as the first branch. The tree now has a rounded apex and a light, floating feel to it.

12 Maintenance of azalea species

This species needs an acidic soil, and as the basic Bonsai soil mix has been used, a proprietary tonic containing chelated iron is added to the soil surface and watered in. This will soon green up the foliage.

13 The completed Bonsai

Although the trunk lacks taper the completed Bonsai has an airy, light feeling to it. Material suited to no other style has been used to create a convincing literati-style Bonsai. Soon the flower buds will open and one will be rewarded with a burst of colour.

Final height of the Bonsai including pot is 28 in. (71 cm.).

Aftercare

After watering, the Bonsai will be given protection from wind and frost. When it has finished flowering the dead flower buds are removed to conserve the tree's energy. It will be allowed to grow freely for the next year.

The future

The wire and raffia will be removed when the branches are set in position (usually the following year). Regular applications of chelated iron will be given to ensure the tree remains healthy. Throughout its future, excess growth is removed to maintain the somewhat sparse foliage mass, to keep the tree from appearing top-heavy.

Project 7   Windswept juniper

An elderly tree, battered by nature

Materials: juniper tree   pot   soil
wound sealant   wire   small paintbrush
sharp knife   white water-soluble paint
cigarette lighter   moss   alpines
lime sulphur   basic tools plus small wire brush

Suitable species: the featured tree is *Juniperus chinensis* 'Kuriwao Gold'. This has a more golden foliage than the normal Chinese Juniper which is used extensively in Bonsai. Almost any of the hundreds of juniper varieties is suitable for this project, as are larch and yew.

Season: this project can be carried out at any time of the year provided sensible aftercare is given. In winter this means the completed Bonsai must be kept frost-free; in late spring or autumn, shading must be given to prevent possible sun scorching and dehydration.

Comments: the chief technique in this project is the creation of dead wood branches (jin) and an area of trunk stripped of bark (shari). The dead wood areas are appropriate in this style of Bonsai as they recreate the harsh environmental conditions that the tree would have undergone in the wild.

1 The materials

There are several new materials required, explained and demonstrated below.

2 Planting angle (1)

The windswept style of Bonsai is a variant of the slanting style. The trunk will be tilted to one side, with all the branches flowing in the same direction.

3 Planting angle (2)

Low branches are shortened; they are not required and will be converted into dead wood jins. The tree is now removed from its container and root-pruned.

4 Planting angle (3)

Now the extraneous lower branches have been shortened, one can see that the best choice is to lean the tree to the right; so that when the low branches are converted to dead wood they will be in view from the front. If the tree were leaned to the left the jins would be obscured by the trunk. A round pot would be a suitable choice for this planting.

5 Choice of pot

An alternative is to use a crescent-shaped pot obtained from a Bonsai supplier. The back of the pot represents a symbolic cliff face and the whole feeling of the tree's harsh history is amplified by this choice of container.

6 Creation of dead wood area (1)

The rootball is wrapped with a damp cloth to protect it and keep the roots moist. The branch stumps are to be converted to dead wood jins. In addition, an area of bark is to be stripped from the trunk of the tree to represent the effects of wind blasting (dead wood on a trunk is known as 'shari'). At this stage it is useful to use white, water-soluble paint to determine the areas that will be stripped of bark. The decision on the extent of the dead wood area is made at this stage.

7 Creation of dead wood area (2)

A sharp knife is used to cut through the bark at the boundary of the area designated to the dead wood.

Project 7   Windswept juniper

8 Creation of dead wood area (3)

The bark is pulled away from the trunk in one continuous strip.

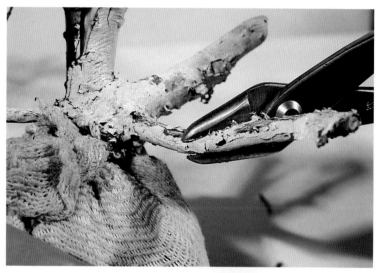

9 Creation of dead wood area (4)

The bark on the dead wood branches is squeezed, with pliers, along their length. This releases the bark from the wood.

104

10 Creation of dead wood area (5)

The bark is easily pulled away from the branches.

11 Creation of dead wood area (6)

The dead area is free of bark. However, it looks fresh and needs sculpting to give an impression of age.

12 Creation of dead wood area (7)

The area now needs refining into something more naturalistic in appearance. The jins are shortened by first cutting half-way into them from behind (thus any tool marks will not show from the front).

13 Creation of dead wood area (8)

The jin end is grasped by the pliers and twisted forwards. This leaves a natural-looking texture in the wood.

14 Creation of dead wood area (9)

The whole dead wood area is shaped by carving. In the photograph a specialist tool, 'wen cutters', is being used. Branch-cutters are suitable; alternatives are small chisels or any other implement that will carve the wood.

15 Creation of dead wood area (10)

Adding shape to the dead wood continues.

16 Creation of dead wood area (10)

The area of dead wood is burnt using a cigarette lighter (a jeweller's blow-torch does the task more efficiently). This burning does not harm the tree as only the dead areas are touched. The burning serves four purposes: it dries out the wood; it removes any small splinters; it smooths the edges left by the carving tools; it produces darker tones in the burnt areas which show through the lime sulphur (which is to be applied) resulting in a different tone that enhances the final appearance.

17 Creation of dead wood area (11)

A small wire brush (such as that for buffing suede shoes) is vigorously rubbed over the burnt area. This removes the charcoal deposits created by the burning and helps to smooth the whole area.

18 Creation of dead wood area (12)

A small hobby drill is used to add the final touches; a small file or sandpaper are alternatives. The area should not be 'polished' as this looks artificial. The carving of the dead wood area is complete.

19 Potting the tree

The tree is wired into the crescent container. The photograph shows that if this is done correctly the pot can be lifted by the trunk!

20 Bleaching the dead wood (1)

The dead wood area must be treated to stop it rotting. Lime sulphur will be painted on to the surface. To begin, the area is sprayed with water which opens up the pores of the wood and helps the lime sulphur penetrate the surface.

Project 7   Windswept juniper

21 Bleaching the dead wood (2)

Lime sulphur is painted on to the surface. The sulphur ingredient preserves the wood and stops it rotting; the lime helps bleach it white giving a natural appearance as of ancient trees. WARNING: take care when using lime sulphur - it has a dreadful odour and should only be used outside. It must be painted on the dead wood only, ensuring that none comes into contact with the living areas or the soil. Over the next few days it will cause the dead wood area to become a subdued white.

22 End of stage one

The dead wood areas are complete, and the tree has been under-planted with some small alpine plants to enhance the rugged atmosphere. Moss has been placed round the edge of the pot to prevent the soil from washing away. Time for a well-earned rest before embarking on pruning and wiring the rest of the tree. This process could be undertaken at a later date if wished.

23 Defining the branches (1)

The branches on the windward side of the tree are to be removed.

24 Refining the branches (2)

The new jins are wired and bent into position. The live branches on the leeward side are also wired and placed. Several of the live branches on this side are also jinned. This all helps to reduce the foliage mass and enhance the rugged appearance. Trees in the wild growing in this style show a spartan appearance due to the ravages of their environment. This atmosphere must be echoed in the Bonsai.

25 Refining the branches (3)

Any branches on the sides of the trunk will be jinned and bent towards the leeward side.

26 Refining the branches (4)

The process of thinning, wiring and positioning the branches continues. Any foliage pointing straight downwards from the live branches is removed, which helps create the floating appearance of the foliage pads.

Project 7   Windswept juniper

27 Refining the branches (4)
The apex of the tree is also
converted to dead wood. All
the branches are now in their
new positions - facing away
from the wind. Small
adjustments to their positions
are made until the completed
image is satisfactory.

28 Dead wood areas
The dead wood in close-up shows a natural
shape and texture. The small jinned upper branches
will set into their new positions as the wood dries.
Alternatively (as in this case) they can be heated
with the flame from the lighter and allowed to
cool. When the wire is removed they will
stay in position.

29 Branch 'clouds'
The branches are pruned and pinched to create
domed, cloud-shaped masses.

30 The completed Bonsai
The one-sided branch structure and under-planting contribute to a stylized but convincing image of a windswept tree. The final task is to shorten some of the jins.

Final height of the Bonsai including pot is 22 in. (56 cm.).

Aftercare

Protection from frost and shade is provided. The foliage is misted daily until new growth appears.

The future

The dead wood areas will be treated with lime sulphur every year. The foliage areas will be kept fairly sparse by pinching out excess growth.

Project 8 Triple-trunk Scots pine

Styling collected material into an elegant clump of old pine trees

Materials: large collected or nursery pine

tools   wire   wound sealant

Suitable species: the featured tree is a Scots Pine collected from the wild. Many nurseries supply large shrubs and trees in containers which would be suitable for this project. Most other species of pine are suitable including Mugo Pine, Black Pine, Mountain Pine and any of the many variants of Scots Pine such as *Beuvronensis*. If large material is unavailable or not practicable then a smaller tree with a similar trunk disposition may be used.

Season: any time of year, though late spring is the optimum.

Comments: the final project demonstrates several new aspects of Bonsai creation.

1 Use of large tree material. To the uninitiated this seems inappropriate for Bonsai. However, it is easier to work with larger material, and the results are impressive.
2 Advanced design considerations.
3 Refinement of pine species.

This Bonsai requires knowledge and understanding of the techniques demonstrated in the previous projects.

1 The tree material (1)

This Scots Pine is approximately 50 years old and was collected three years before from a heathland site. It has been allowed to regenerate its strength since the trauma of collection and is now healthy and vigorous. It has a very pleasing distribution of trunks. Although the second and third trunks are, in reality, upright growing branches, they will be used to create a triple-trunk-style Bonsai.

2 The tree material (2)

The tree has been lightly root-pruned and planted in a round pot. This style of pot is called 'primitive' due to its natural texture and lack of glazing - it suits this tree very well. A healthy pine will often have a covering of white fungus called 'mycorrhiza' on its roots (see Looking after Bonsai - Pests and Diseases, page 127); this is beneficial to the pine but should not be confused with root aphids which are a pest. The mycorrhiza is distinguishable by its creamy colour, frond texture and distinctive 'earthy' smell; the root aphids are more blue-white in colour.

3 Removal of lower branches (1)

The image to be created is of an old clump of mature pines. Scots Pines (and many other pines) shed their lower branches as they get older resulting in the familiar tall trunk with a mop of foliage at the apex. These lower branches are much too long; they will be shortened or removed altogether.

4 Removal of lower branches (2)

It is often difficult to visualize the result of removing branches. A tip: temporarily covering those branches with a cloth may help you make the decision. With these branches obscured the tree has undergone a transformation - it has gained an elegance and 'age' much more in keeping with its mature relatives in the wild. The choice of front of the tree has also been made: this view gives the best distribution of the trunks. A white label has been placed in the pot to mark the front and act as a reminder.

5 Removal of lower branches (3)

Side view - the excess lower branches are removed leaving stubs. These stubs are now jinned and may be used for the anchorage of wires later on. Pruning cuts should be sealed with the wound sealant to prevent excess leakage of sap. Work now starts to decide the height of the finished Bonsai.

6 Determining the height (1)

The three trunks differ in thickness, which creates a more natural feeling. Each trunk will be styled as a separate tree, while ensuring that the 'three' trees marry together to create a single image. The middle trunk is thickest and strongest and so it is natural to make this the tallest tree with the other two trunks subordinate. The right-hand trunk is too tall and must be reduced in height.

Project 8   Triple-trunk Scots pine

7 Determining the height (2)

The original apex has been removed and this smaller branch will be wired upwards to create a new apex to that trunk. This process has also induced a better taper to the top of the trunk. The left-hand trunk is reduced in the same way.

8 Determining the height (3)

Now that the height of the subsidiary trunks has been determined the height of the central trunk must be decided. The trunk splits into two - the left-hand trunk is straight and the right-hand one is curved. Keeping both would make the finished Bonsai look top heavy, so one must be removed - but which one?

9 Determining the height (4)

The curved trunk would look out of place on the finished Bonsai - there would appear an apparent kink at the top of the trunk. Before removal the technique of using a cloth to obscure it is used to assess the Bonsai's appearance afterwards.

10 Determining the height (5)

The curved trunk has been removed.

11 Determining the height (6)

The straight trunk is wired upwards. Now the final height has been decided. The top of the Bonsai has also been lightened by this process and it is already looking far more tree-like. The major design decisions have been made and acted upon; the next stage is to wire and refine all the branches.

12 Positioning of secondary trunk

The left-hand trunk is a little too close to the central trunk. It has been re-positioned by using one of the jins as a bracer for a piece of wire to move it slightly to one side. This unobtrusive technique alleviates the need for heavy-gauge wire on the trunk.

Project 8   Triple-trunk Scots pine

13 Refining the image - technique 1

The branches and all the subsidiary twigs are wired and placed into rounded or spade shapes when viewed from above. Many curves are introduced when the twigs are placed in position as this adds the appearance of age.

14 Refining the image - technique 2

Any twigs that point straight downwards are removed, as are any that are over-long.

15 Refining the image - technique 3

Old needles are pulled from the branches and twigs. This has two effects - it reduces the 'juvenile' appearance of the tree and it helps the production of new buds.

16 Refining the image

Progressing up the trunks these three techniques are used to lighten the foliage and position the branches and shape them. Over the next two years the tree will produce many new buds which will increase the density of the foliage on the branches.

17 Refining the apex (1)

The last step is to refine the apex of each of the trunks. The central trunk is worked on first.

18 Refining the apex (2)

The central trunk after it has been wired and shaped. It has a rounded, more tree-like appearance with each branch occupying a different spatial position.

119

Project 8   Triple-trunk Scots pine

19 Refining the apex (3)
The apex of each of the other two trunks has been refined in the same way.

20 The completed Bonsai (1)
The Bonsai process has produced an elegant, refined image.

21 The completed Bonsai (2)
The side view shows how the Bonsai is three-dimensional with back branches, and the trunks tilt slightly forwards.

Final height of the Bonsai including pot is 35 in. (89 cm.).

Aftercare

Normal aftercare of a protected environment and regular misting is provided until the tree is producing new growth. Pines prefer a slightly drier soil than most other species so watering is less frequent.

The future

The branches will set in their new positions during the next two years. A close watch is kept for the wire biting in and it is removed if this starts to occur. The tree will be allowed to grow freely during that time to re-vitalize itself after the rigours of the styling exercise, and to help the branches set in position. The tree is only lightly fertilized from now on to keep it healthy but without encouraging unwanted sappy growth. When the wire has been removed the new growth (called 'candles') will be shortened each year (see Pruning). The density of the branches will be developed, but if the tree 'closes in' and starts to resemble a dwarf conifer then it will be groomed by removing excess growth to retain the elegant image.

Project 8   Triple-trunk Scots pine

3

Maintaining and displaying Bonsai

Looking after Bonsai

A Bonsai, like any tree, needs light, water, nutrients and some protection from threats such as sun scorch, frost, pests and diseases, for its continued well-being.

Bonsai are watered using a fine-spray nozzle attachment to a hosepipe or watering-can. Periodically the whole pot is submerged in water for half-an-hour. Tall cascade pots are best watered using both methods.

Watering

Bonsai, like all plants, need water. But how often to water? Water is given as often as the tree requires it. When the weather is hot, more water is lost through the leaves by transpiration, so the frequency of watering is increased. When the tree is dormant in the winter the water requirement diminishes, so the frequency of watering is reduced.

Each Bonsai has a different water requirement, depending on species, local environment, size, soil type and container size. Therefore, there is no hard and fast rule on how often to water. Start by watering on a daily basis. If the soil is continually damp then lessen the frequency. It is a matter of observation and common sense, but the great bonus of using a free-draining soil is that it is near impossible to over-water, so the danger of root rot is virtually eliminated.

Watering tips

Start by watering daily, then reduce the frequency if the soil is still damp.

After an initial watering-in, do not water newly repotted Bonsai until the soil starts to dry, which indicates the root system is active and has recovered from root-pruning.

Mains water is quite adequate, but in an area of very hard water apply chelated iron to lime-hating plants such as azaleas.

In the summer, water even if it has been raining. This may bring a smile to the faces of neighbours, but it needs to be done. A large canopy of leaves will act as an umbrella and shelter the soil from the rain.

It is sensible periodically to immerse the whole pot in a large container of water and leave it for between two and ten minutes: this ensures any 'dry spots' in the pot receive water.

Use a fine-spray nozzle and water over the leaf canopy as well. This helps remove dust and grime, and if you are watering in the evening the leaves absorb some of this water throughout the night. A fine spray also prevents the soil being washed out of the pot.

Water early in the evening as first choice, and early morning as second choice. Midday watering can result in leaf scorch as the droplets of water act as tiny magnifying glasses.

If you grow very small Bonsai they may require watering several times a day in the heat of the summer.

Watering is not a chore: rather it brings one into daily contact with one's Bonsai, a time for inspection, a relaxing period at the end of the day.

If you enlist someone to water for you when you are away make sure they are reliable and have been shown how to water the Bonsai properly.

If in doubt, over-water rather than under-water. The porous soil recommended for Bonsai will drain freely.

Fertilizer

Bonsai require nutrients. These must be given by the grower. Granular fertilizers are preferred to soluble ones as they break down slowly and provide a constant trickle of feed at each watering. Also, it is very easy to overdo it with soluble fertilizers - 'killing by kindness'. Fertilizer is given to promote growth and health, but a Bonsai which has been lightly fertilized and allowed to grow and develop slowly will have thinner twigs and a more natural appearance. If too much fertilizer is given the new shoots will have long internodes - that is, a greater distance between the nodes, or leaf junctions. This is undesirable: the Bonsai grower is seeking a tight, twiggy growth pattern when building up the ramification of the branches.

Bonsai are supplied with nutrients by spreading a little granular fertilizer on the soil surface three times a year. This meets the requirements of the majority of Bonsai including this unusual gooseberry Bonsai which sets fruit every year. If a lime-hating species, such as an azalea, develops chlorosis (a yellowing of the leaves), then a fertilizer containing chelated iron is used.

Section 3   Maintaining and displaying Bonsai

I have experimented with many fertilizers and my conclusions are as follows:

Use granular, slow-release fertilizers. Any of the proprietary ones are fine.

Give less, rather than more. A half-teaspoon per 25 cm. pot spread over the soil surface three times a year, in spring, summer and autumn, is sufficient.

Balanced feeds are best. Look for the three figures on the fertilizer packet: these should be the same or similar, e.g. 5-5-5. They indicate the ratios of nitrogen, phosphorous and potash content.

Flowering species require more potash, so give a fertilizer with a higher potash rating, e.g. 5-5-10.

Fertilizers with added magnesium, such as rose fertilizers, are very good for Bonsai. I have had success with fertilizers containing a chemical called En Mag. This contains additional magnesium; furthermore it does not release lime into the soil when it breaks down, so is suitable for lime-haters such as azaleas.

Experiment with several fertilizers, then stick to two or three that work for you and rotate their application.

Organic fertilizers are just as good as man-made ones.

Do not be seduced into hastening the refinement stage of a Bonsai by using very high-nitrogen fertilizers that appear to offer fast growth. The new growth is undesirably sappy and lengthy. These fertilizers can be used to build bulk rapidly, but should always be used with caution.

Placement - a healthy environment

Where a Bonsai is positioned profoundly affects its health and wellbeing. In the wild a tree will usually grow where the environmental conditions are suitable. Bonsai have no control over their localized environment, so the grower must be sensitive to their placement.

Bonsai should be sited outside where the light levels are high and there is a good flow of fresh air. A large amount of space is not required - many people who live in flats and apartments successfully keep Bonsai on either a balcony or a rooftop.

All Bonsai need to be sited where there is a good air flow. Slow, stagnant air results in all sorts of problems, notably mildew.

It is always safer to keep Bonsai frost-free. Light frosts do little damage. Hard frosts, however, can freeze the soil and the roots. The water in the roots turns to ice and expands and ruptures the root walls (in the same way as water pipes burst when frozen).

Pines and junipers, being trees of the mountains, require high light levels and should be given full sun. Most other species appreciate a little light shading from the heat of the summer sun. Plastic netting is a good material with which to build an overhead canopy.

If Bonsai are sited near a wall or fence they should be turned every few days or else the growth will be imbalanced (the shaded side of the tree will grow less).

Pests and diseases

At one time or another all Bonsai will be attacked by something that will harm them, whether it be insects, disease or the local wildlife. Most trees in the wild harbour some pests with little damage: the size and vigour of the tree provides strength and resilience. I once cut a small branch from a mature sycamore tree growing in the wild, to photograph it for a magazine article I was preparing, and was astonished to count eight different insect species on five leaves, but the tree appeared to be healthy and suffering no ill-effects. However, a Bonsai is stunted and has less resistance to attacks.

A watch needs to be kept for pests and diseases. Insecticides and fungicide treatments are applied only if the situation is getting out of hand, or if the Bonsai is to be exhibited. In many instances a strong jet of water from a hose is all that is required to dislodge the majority of pests. Many proprietary chemical sprays and treatments are not designed for use on trees and their reaction can sometimes be harmful. On Bonsai always use any treatment at the lowest recommended strength.

Fungicide treatments should never be applied to the soil unless for an exceptional reason. Many species of tree have a beneficial fungus, mycorrhiza, which acts in a symbiotic relationship with tree roots and helps them absorb nutrients. Applying certain fungicides to the soil could kill the mycorrhiza.

127

Repotting Bonsai

A Bonsai is repotted when its roots have filled the container, and it is becoming pot-bound. The frequency depends on several factors - size of the pot, age, vigour of the Bonsai, and climatic conditions. In general, a young vigorous Bonsai is repotted every year or two; as it ages the frequency reduces. The root system is inspected annually and if there is still ample space for the roots to grow it is not repotted.

Repotting is normally done when the new season's buds are swelling in early to mid-spring. The actual time of year when the buds swell depends largely on the climate and the species; it may vary from year to year according to the severity of the previous winter. In practice this means that some species of Bonsai require repotting at an earlier time than others. For example, many of the maples leaf out up to three months before beech. The key to determining the correct time for repotting is to watch the buds for signs of swelling. Evergreens such as pines are also best repotted during the spring.

The repotting sequence for an established Bonsai is the same as that demonstrated in Project 1 except that only one third of the rootball is removed during the root-pruning.

Emergency treatment for sick Bonsai

If Bonsai sicken then it is vital to ascertain the cause. In many cases this will be far from obvious. Most tree and shrub species are fairly resilient, but they will benefit from a helping hand to assist recovery. The following guidelines will help to minimize losses.

1   DO NOT FERTILIZE - remove any fertilizer still on the soil surface.
2   If you suspect that excess fertilizing is the cause then place the potted Bonsai in a container of water that just comes to the rim of the pot and trickle water into the container from a hose or tap continuously for 24 hours, allowing the excess to flow away. This process will help leech out the fertilizer.
3   If the foliage has wilted due to drought DO NOT IMMERSE THE POT. Too much water given too quickly may cause rupturing of cells within the plant. Instead, give a little water from a hose or watering-can and leave in a shaded, wind-proof area for half-an-hour and repeat several times. After a few hours the whole pot can be immersed in water for an hour.
4   If the cause appears to be pests or diseases treat with a proprietary spray.
5   If there appears to be no obvious cause then remove the Bonsai from its pot and inspect the root system. If the soil smells 'sour' and the roots are mushy then root rot is probably the cause. Any 'maggots' with orange-coloured heads are vine weevil larvae and they may have eaten the fine feeder-roots of the tree. In either case wash the whole root system; cut off any damaged root ends and seal the cuts with wound sealant; then plant in 100 per cent fine grit, water in, and give aftercare as per a freshly root-pruned Bonsai. Wait until the next spring before repotting into normal Bonsai soil. If vine weevil was the cause then dunk the whole of the repotted Bonsai in a solution containing Gamma-HCH.
6   In all cases provide a protected, but airy, environment, free from direct sun and frost. Mist the foliage and twigs to help with water intake and the production of new buds.
7   If all else fails and no cause has been found then provide a protected environment and hope for the best.

Keeping records

Maintaining a record of one's Bonsai trees is an excellent idea. It provides a history of maintenance and training, and is invaluable when reviewing their progress. Keeping a brief written record is not time-consuming and, while it might seem slightly bureaucratic, it is all part of the hobby of Bonsai.

The following form includes all the information that should be recorded, one sheet for each Bonsai. In addition a few photographs filed with the record sheet also help one check on progress and development. Photographs do not have to be of special quality - a simple 'snap' is all that is needed.

Species .... Number in collection ....

Source: Propagation/Nursery Stock/Collected/Bonsai Supplier/Other:
    Cost .... Date Acquired .... Pot .... Height .... Trunk diameter ....
Removed From Collection: Date .... Reason: Sold/Gift/Died

---

Year 1 ....
Height............Trunk diameter ....Photographed Date ....Repotted: Y/N Root-pruned: Y/N Change of pot Y/N
Fungicide treatment dates .... Insecticide treatment dates ....
Fertiliser: Type ....Date ....Type .... Date .... Type .... Date............
Training: Wire applied Date .... Wire removal Date .... Major pruning Date............
Exhibited: Where .... Date .... Where .... Date............
Notes for next year ....

Year 2 ....
Height............Trunk diameter ....Photographed Date ....Repotted: Y/N Root-pruned: Y/N Change of pot Y/N
Fungicide treatment dates .... Insecticide treatment dates ....
Fertiliser: Type ....Date ....Type .... Date .... Type .... Date............
Training: Wire applied Date .... Wire removal Date .... Major pruning Date............
Exhibited: Where .... Date .... Where .... Date............
Notes for next year ....

Year 3 ....
Height............Trunk diameter ....Photographed Date ....Repotted: Y/N Root-pruned: Y/N Change of pot Y/N
Fungicide treatment dates .... Insecticide treatment dates ....
Fertiliser: Type ....Date............Type .... Date .... Type .... Date............
Training: Wire applied Date .... Wire removal Date .... Major pruning Date............
Exhibited: Where .... Date .... Where .... Date............
Notes for next year ....

Year 4 ....
Height............Trunk diameter ....Photographed Date ....Repotted: Y/N Root-pruned: Y/N Change of pot Y/N
Fungicide treatment dates .... Insecticide treatment dates ....
Fertiliser: Type ....Date ....Type .... Date .... Type .... Date............
Training: Wire applied Date .... Wire removal Date .... Major pruning Date............
Exhibited: Where .... Date .... Where .... Date............
Notes for next year ....

Year 5 ....
Height............Trunk diameter ....Photographed Date ....Repotted: Y/N Root-pruned: Y/N Change of pot Y/N
Fungicide treatment dates .... Insecticide treatment dates ....
Fertiliser: Type ....Date............Type .... Date .... Type .... Date............
Training: Wire applied Date .... Wire removal Date .... Major pruning Date............
Exhibited: Where .... Date .... Where .... Date............
Notes for next year ....

---

notes

Section 3   Maintaining and displaying Bonsai

Displaying Bonsai

You have now created a Bonsai collection: your thoughts must turn to where they will be kept. The ideal Bonsai display area both meets the horticultural needs of the Bonsai and shows them off so they may be appreciated.

Display ideas

On special occasions the Japanese traditionally display Bonsai in small alcoves at the entrance to the home - these are called 'Tokonoma'. A Bonsai is brought into the house for a few days and displayed with a scroll painting, or perhaps a viewing stone.

Bonsai are usually displayed the year round on wooden benches in the garden. The benches serve a double purpose: in the winter the Bonsai can be placed under them and a covering such as polythene laid over the top of the bench and draped down over the sides to the ground where it forms a mini-greenhouse - this gives good protection from all but the hardest frosts.

Another way of displaying Bonsai is on 'monkey poles'. These are wooden or stone plinths with a small platform on the top. A single Bonsai is displayed on each pole.

130

The poles are set at different heights which helps each Bonsai to be appreciated individually, whereas on a bench the eye tends to wander from one to another. A simple raised platform display can be achieved using a few concrete blocks on top of one another and then a small paving slab placed on top. For extra stability the whole structure can be cemented together. However, left free-standing these simple displays can be disassembled, and reassembled at a different location very easily.

A Bonsai display at the UK National Convention. The plinths are sited at different heights and positions which allows each tree to be viewed and appreciated on its own. Under-plantings of complementary foliage plants and an Oriental stone lantern complete the picture. This method of displaying Bonsai can be adopted by the Bonsai-grower within the confines of the garden to show a collection off at its finest.

A small oriental-style garden can be constructed with minimum effort by building a few display plinths and laying some attractive gravel underneath. A bamboo screen as a backdrop and a couple of small shrubs or plants set into the gravel complete an attractive small Bonsai display.

Many people enjoy fish-keeping as a complementary hobby to Bonsai and site their trees next to a pond. The sound of running water certainly adds atmosphere to the display.

A good method of displaying one's ever-increasing Bonsai collection is to construct a small, but more lavish area for the best Bonsai so that they can be shown and appreciated to full effect. A secondary, simpler area of benching is used for the trees in training and raw material.

Ideally, any display should show the Bonsai at eye-level where they look their best.

Display requirements

Any type of display must be built with a thought to the horticultural needs of the Bonsai. Shading is often required to prevent summer sun scorching. This can be achieved by building a wooden slatted roof or suspending a netting material over the display; either of these act also as a partial barrier against frost.

A site with good air movement (but not too windy) is also required. Stagnant air is bad for the foliage of trees as it encourages mildew and some pests. Too windy a location will also damage the leaves, and the trees may get blown over altogether.

If displays are built close to walls and fences the Bonsai should be rotated every few days to ensure all parts of the tree receive light and so prevent any lop-sided growth.

Whatever display is chosen it must elevate the trees above ground level; otherwise the drainage holes in the pots will provide an entrance for all sorts of pests and unwanted visitors.

Security

It is a sad fact of life that the increase in popularity and public awareness of Bonsai has resulted in temptation for the unscrupulous few to steal them.

The majority of losses are casual opportunist thefts, and it is against these that precautions should be taken. Keeping Bonsai out of sight from the road helps, as does ensuring that access to the rear of one's property is restricted. Three of the most successful security controls are: keeping a dog as a deterrent; installing a light with an infra-red heat or movement sensor; and fitting an alarm system. Any one of these should minimize the risk of Bonsai being stolen.

Insurance cover for Bonsai can sometimes be organized through insurance companies who will cover them under the household policy. However, this is often quite difficult to arrange and valuations will probably be needed. If you have created the Bonsai yourself a sensible assessment of value must be made. Some Bonsai nurserymen will be happy to provide a written valuation, particularly if you frequent their nurseries for the purchase of Bonsai tools and supplies.

Ornaments and figurines

Some people like to place ornaments and figurines either within a Bonsai pot or next to it to enhance the oriental atmosphere. This is a matter of personal taste, but any such objects should be removed before exhibiting a Bonsai.

Accent plantings

An excellent accompaniment to a Bonsai is an accent planting. A small flowering plant, grass or fern is planted in a small pot on its own and placed near the Bonsai. The Japanese have raised accent plantings to an art form, and when sympathetically done an accent planting provides a more tasteful accompaniment to a Bonsai than a figurine.

In this formal Bonsai display, a literati-style Scots Pine, a small accent planting and a viewing-stone all complement each other and create an atmosphere of spring.

Viewing-stones

No book on the subject of Bonsai would be complete without mentioning the companion topic, viewing-stones or 'Suiseki'. Displays of Bonsai are often accompanied by viewing-stones and many enthusiasts enjoy both. Stones and rocks play an important part in Bonsai. They are used in several styles such as rock plantings and root-over-rock style, and are often placed in pots where a more rugged style of planting is required, such as in the windswept style (note that any found rock or stone MUST be thoroughly washed to remove potential pollutants before being placed in a Bonsai pot). Many of those who enjoy Bonsai also appreciate rock and stone for their natural beauty. However, a *suiseki* is much more than an interesting stone or rock and its beauty is best appreciated when displayed on a purpose-designed, hand-crafted wooden stand or dai.

Suiseki (pronounced su-ee-sek-ee) are small, naturally formed rocks and stones that resemble an object such as an animal, or have the power to suggest a scene in miniature, for example a mountain range or an island. *Suiseki* are often referred to as 'viewing-stones' or 'landscape stones'. Although any natural image conjured up by the appearance of the stone would itself be a *suiseki*, the stones most often collected and favoured in the West are those resembling a single mountain or an entire mountain range. The term 'suiseki' is used (in the same way as the word Bonsai) to describe both the art form and the individual stone itself.

The origins of *suiseki* go back nearly 2000 years to China, where these small stones of great beauty had special significance for Buddhist and Taoist followers. The name *suiseki* is formed from two Japanese characters, sui ('water') and seki ('stone'), hence 'water-stones' - stones created by the erosive action of water in streams, rivers and lakes. *Suiseki* can also be formed by any erosive action, for example wind, heat and ice. Some of the Desert *suiseki* formed by 'sand blasting' are magnificent.

Bonsai and *suiseki* are complementary art forms and share many characteristics. In recent years the upsurge of interest in oriental art forms has given a major boost to the practice and popularity of Bonsai, and although *suiseki* is still behind Bonsai in terms of the number of practitioners, it is rapidly gaining popularity.

A magnificent viewing-stone from California, imported into the UK where the owner has lavished over 60 hours of work on designing and carving the hardwood stand.

A distant mountain-view *suiseki* collected from a stream in Dartmoor, UK.

Section 4 Case studies

Over the past years I have had the pleasure of shaping hundreds of Bonsai trees. The majority have been created from raw material, either purchased from nurseries and garden centres or collected from the wild. Some were commissions I received for existing Bonsai trees that needed a change either due to their health or because they had outgrown their current style. Experience is the greatest teacher, and I found my skills and success at creating Bonsai grew in proportion to the number of trees I worked on. Without doubt many of my early efforts were rather poor, and one of the motivations for writing this book is to pass on certain experiences to enable you, the reader, to short-circuit some of the early frustrations.

The case studies contained in this chapter have been chosen to illustrate various design and aesthetic aspects, or techniques that have not been covered in the Projects. Some of the 'before' photographs were taken under working conditions, hence their imperfect technical quality.

I hope that the transformations shown in this chapter also prove inspirational.

A windswept hawthorn

species	*Crataegus monogyna*
common name	common hawthorn
Bonsai style	semi-cascade - windswept
source	collected from a limestone hillside
current age	over 60 years
trained since	1987

This hawthorn Bonsai has given me tremendous pleasure over the years. I was profoundly influenced for its styling by the craggy, ancient hawthorn trees I had seen in the Snowdonia region of North Wales, where environmental effects and continual grazing by sheep have created very memorable images.

The naturalness of the twisted trunks and dense foliage was remarkable, but how should I develop it into a Bonsai? My decisions were based partly on the fact that it had very few roots due to the difficulty of collection from the limestone hillside it had been growing on. There were hundreds of buds waiting to open, and I felt sure the tree would not survive with such a reduced root system. I decided, therefore, to reduce the number of trunks and simplify the whole image. This was achieved by turning the tree on its side and isolating the main trunk line. Two of the residual trunks were stripped of bark and jinned; I also carved them quite extensively to complement the overall effect.

A dramatic Bonsai 'in the flesh', not least as it is 47 in. (120 cm.) from the base to the foliage tip. It flowers every spring, a welcome bonus.

The inspiration and the material for this Bonsai have come from nature. I have merely lent a hand in refining it to its present form.

136

An amazing array of twisted trunks and branches in the raw material.

Detail of the two main carved
branches, or jins.

Seven years after styling into its
current shape. It has been
potted into a tall cascade pot
which suits the ruggedness of
the style very well.

Section 4   Case studies

Case study 2 A mighty honeysuckle

species	*Lonicera nitida*
common name	dwarf honeysuckle
Bonsai style	formal upright
source	an old garden hedge
current age	over 40 years
trained since	1989

Originally part of a garden hedge, this transformation illustrates the potential of what may be found close at hand. The dwarf honeysuckle has tiny evergreen leaves, and buds profusely. In styling the tree I focused on its strongest asset - a very stable, well-defined root buttress - so as to create a short, very powerful, formal, upright Bonsai. The height has been reduced from 48 in. (122 cm.) to 16 in. (40 cm.) and the top carved out to create a dramatic taper.

138

Five years after its initial styling, it is becoming a handsome Bonsai.

Originally part of a mature garden hedge, the solid root buttress can be seen at the base of the trunk.

An 'ancient' yew

species	*Taxus baccata*
common name	yew
Bonsai style	informal upright
source	nursery
current age	approximately 15 years
trained since	1989

Very typical and readily obtainable nursery material, still wrapped in hessian (burlap), a relic of the time it was lifted from the ground the previous year. After a day's work in removing excess branches and foliage the final form emerges. It has now assumed the semblance of a mature, statuesque tree. A mental picture of trees in the countryside has influenced the design.

Although this tree is only about fifteen years old, it now looks much older. The semblance of age, although illusory, has been achieved by repositioning the branches and clearing the trunk of distracting shoots and twigs so that the taper of the trunk can be fully appreciated.

It demonstrates well the fact that the creation of Bonsai is often a matter of subtraction - removing excess material to expose the natural lines hidden within.

139

Typical of material from a nursery - somewhere in this tangle of foliage is a Bonsai waiting to be born.

Eight hours' pruning and wiring, and the Bonsai has been discovered.

Case study 4 Restyling a white pine Bonsai

species	*Pinus pentaphylla*
common name	Japanese white pine
Bonsai style	informal upright
source	Japan
current age	40 years
restyled in	1992

In Japan the white pine is used extensively for Bonsai. Many hundreds of specimens are imported from Japan each year and sold by Bonsai nurseries throughout the world. Many, as in this case, have been grafted onto black pine stock (the graft junction of this Bonsai is just below the first branch). Unfortunately, the white pine does sometimes have a tendency suddenly to sicken and, if no action is taken, the Bonsai may be lost altogether. The first signs of deterioration are all the needles turning a yellow/brown colour. If this is confined to one or two branches only I have found that removing these branches often saves the tree.

The bottom left-hand branch has progressively weakened and is dying. It needs to be removed.

Having studied the tree from all angles I decided to reverse its viewing position - the old front is now the back. A higher branch is going to be lowered to help lessen the gap (using the technique illustrated in Project 5). All the branches will be shortened a little to help with the overall appearance.

The restyling completed: a vastly different appearance, which necessitated a change of pot the following year.

Section 4 Case studies

Twin-trunk hemlock

species	*Tsuga heterophylla*
common name	hemlock
Bonsai style	twin trunk
source	collected from the wild
current age	40 years
trained since	1992

Hemlock species are easily trained into Bonsai. This example demonstrates how the size of the two trunks should differ in this style. A useful training technique is being used here - the smaller trunk has been bent outwards and then straightened by placing a small block of wood between the trunks and then pulling the two trunks towards each other near the top. This is a simple and easy method of removing or adding a bend to old trunks which would be difficult to bend using wire.

Spotted growing in tall grass, this naturally stunted hemlock has the potential to be a Bonsai.

Two years later, after considerable pruning and wiring, the final form has emerged.

Case study 6 Broom-style zelkova

species	*Zelkova serrata*
common name	Japanese grey bark elm
Bonsai style	broom
source	imported from Japan in the early 1980s
current age	over 40 years
trained since	1985

The zelkova is used extensively by the Japanese to create this newest of Bonsai styles - the broom style, so called due to its resemblance to an upturned broom. Of all Bonsai styles, high-quality trees of this style are perhaps the nearest in appearance to actual trees of the countryside.

I acquired the tree, originally imported from Japan, in 1985, when it was over 30 years old. It already had the basic branch structure but required much more ramification. Over the years I concentrated on exposing the root buttress and building up the very twiggy canopy. As with all the finest deciduous Bonsai zelkova are best appreciated in the winter months when the fine tracery of twigs can be enjoyed without being obscured by the leaves.

The fine twigs are developed and encouraged by fertilizing and watering only sparingly during the spring and early summer. This prevents the tree from issuing long sappy growth. At 18 in. (46 cm.) tall it is an excellent size for displaying and has been exhibited in many Bonsai shows.

A lovely broom-style Bonsai with good rootage, a solid straight trunk and detailed ramification.

Korean hornbeam

species	*Carpinus turczaninowii*
common name	Korean hornbeam
Bonsai style	informal upright
source	imported from Japan in 1987
current age	approximately 35 years
restyled in	1988

This Bonsai illustrates the increase in apparent age achieved by shortening and rounding the apex. Already trained in Japan, this small Bonsai had many fine attributes - stable radiating rootage, a good trunk taper and the basis of a twiggy branch structure. However, the tree gave an appearance of youth due to its very conical shape. I removed the top 3 in. (8 cm.) of trunk to create a more rounded, natural apex and encouraged the ramification of the twigs over the next few years. Although a little of the taper has been lost this will be regained as the tree gets older.

144

The original Bonsai imported from Japan. The triangular shape and pointed apex give an impression of youth.

After removing the existing apex and re-growing the top branches, the more rounded image has resulted in an appearance of increased age.

Section 4   Case studies

Literati pine

species	*Pinus sylvestris*
common name	Scots pine
Bonsai style	literati - triple-trunk
source	collected from the wild
current age	approximately 100 years
styled in	1992

While still at an early stage of its training into a Bonsai, this Scots pine is already showing tremendous promise. It is an old tree which I collected for its natural beauty and Bonsai potential.

It has a shallow root system and was easily removed from its growing site by cutting around the root-ball and lifting it out of the ground. After a year was allowed for it to stabilize in a large container, it was styled and repotted into a Bonsai pot. The styling took two days as all the branches had to be wired and placed in very precise positions. Also, the left-hand trunk has had a 180-degree bend introduced into it to lower its position and provide additional interest in terms of its shape. Bending a trunk of this age and size takes a determined effort!

Many years' work lie ahead in refining the branches which will entail some being removed so that the whole appearance has a light, floating feel to it, so essential in this style of Bonsai.

It is an excellent example of quality being more important than size in Bonsai. How tall do you think it is?

Growing in a boggy area this pine is very old, but the poor soil environment has stunted its growth.

A literati-style Scots pine for the future.

English elm

species	*Ulmus procera*
common name	English elm
Bonsai style	'natural' or formal upright
source	collected from the wild
current age	approximately 35 years
styled in	1990

I acquired this potential Bonsai from a supplier who had in turn purchased it from a Bonsai enthusiast. It had been collected and planted back in the ground and grown and clipped each year for several years. When I acquired it the branches were over a metre in length and its appearance was reminiscent of an aged oak tree. Because oaks are so difficult to train into Bonsai I decided that this would be a good opportunity to create an aged 'oak' Bonsai. The rootage and branch structure are excellent and it is now going through a stage of refinement of the branch ramification.

Due to the ravages of Dutch elm disease, it is now rare to see a mature English elm in the British countryside, so what better way to enjoy this lovely species than to grow one as a Bonsai?

An English elm grown in a very natural style, reminiscent of a mature oak tree.

Case study 10 Driftwood-style juniper

species	*Juniperus media* x *blaauwii*
common name	Blaauws juniper
Bonsai style	driftwood (by wrap-around technique)
source	nursery stock plant
current age	approximately 10 years
styled in	1989

This is a sculptural style of Bonsai. The wrap-around technique is a good method of achieving a dramatic driftwood-style Bonsai without the need to use carving implements. The Bonsai is created by attaching a young sapling to an existing piece of interesting-shaped dead wood. The wood is cleaned and a slot cut into the back of it where the trunk of the sapling will sit. The wood is then bleached with lime sulphur and allowed to dry; and then the trunk of the sapling is pushed into the slot. It is held firmly in position with tape and wire. As the trunk expands it fills the slot and marries itself to the driftwood creating a single entity. The foliage of the tree is then wired and shaped.

Driftwood style Bonsai created by the wrap-around technique.

Detail of the back of the Bonsai
showing the placement of the
original stock plant.

Supplemental information

Species guide

Many species of tree and shrub may be used for Bonsai. This species guide is a brief synopsis with an assessment of the suitability of each for its use as Bonsai material. In the space available it simply is not possible to list every species or all their attributes, so the focus has been placed on assessing the merits of species that are regularly stocked by garden centres, nurseries and other similar outlets.

Name

Listed in alphabetical order by Latin name, with the common name in brackets.

Suitability

The overall suitability for Bonsai evaluated out of five. One star * suggests poor Bonsai material, whereas five stars ***** is best of all.

Beginners

Also rated out of five stars, but this time in relation to the ease of use by a beginner at Bonsai. For example, some species are excellent for Bonsai, but are more demanding either in horticultural requirements or training methods.

Comments

Any pertinent comments or additional information.

Abies (fir)

suitability   **
beginner   **

Comments
Leaves almost succulent. Poor bark texture on many varieties.

Acer (maple)

Many species including *A. buergerianum* (trident maple) and *A. palmatum* (mountain maple).

suitability   *****
beginner   *****

Comments
Good all-round Bonsai material. Watch for virus infections and mildew on trident maple. Summer shading needs to be provided for all varieties.

Berberis

suitability   ***
beginner   **

Comments
Most species small-leaved, some evergreen. Very sharp thorns on many varieties make it difficult (and sometimes painful) to train.

Betula (birch)

Silver birch and Arctic birch most commonly available.

suitability   ****
beginner   ****

Comments
Tough and easy, well worth trying, particularly the Arctic birch which has tiny leaves.

Buxus (box)

suitability   ***
beginner   ***

Comments
Small-leaved, used for hedging. Best developed by pruning rather than wiring.

Carpinus (hornbeam)

suitability   *****
beginner   *****

Comments
Often confused with beech (hornbeam has serrated leaf margins; beech are undulating but smooth). Readily produces buds around large pruning cuts. All varieties (except fastigiate) suitable.

Cedrus (cedar)

suitability   ****
beginner   ****

Comments
Wide availability and attractive needle-like foliage make this good starting Bonsai material.

Chaenomeles (quince)

suitability   ***
beginner   **

Comments
Popular in Japan. Beautiful flowers.

Chamaecyparis (false cypress)
Hinoki cypress (C. obtusa) only.

suitability   *
beginner   **

Comments
High availability and wide choice. Ultimately poor Bonsai material - does not bud back well and is 'leggy'.

Corylus (hazel)

suitability   **
beginner   **

Comments
Many better genera than this, but the variety 'Contorta' is a natural literati and worth trying, if only for its fascinating natural growth habit.

Cotoneaster

suitability   ***
beginner   *****

Comments
Small-leaved, tough, many varieties flower and set fruit. Ideal beginner tree.

Crataegus (hawthorn)

suitability   *****
beginner   ****

Comments
Collected specimens of the common hawthorn (*C. monogyna*) make superb Bonsai with interesting trunks, small leaves and lovely white spring-time flowers. Many other suitable varieties.

Cryptomeria (Japanese cedar)

suitability   ***
beginner   *

Comments
Difficult for beginners - die-back of foliage a problem and quite temperamental.

Euonymous (spindle tree)

suitability   **
beginner   **

Comments
The 'winged' bark is a most attractive feature.

Fagus (beech)

suitability   *****
beginner   *****

Comments
Sold for hedging and very easy to find. Excellent for forest and group Bonsai. *Nothofagus* (false beech) is a separate genus, but also very good as Bonsai material.

Fraxinus (ash)

suitability   *
beginner   *

Comments
Large compound leaves, not well suited to the Bonsai process.

Fruit trees (apple, pear, plum, etc.)

suitability   **
beginner   **

Comments
Can make interesting Bonsai, but most have bad grafts.

Ginkgo (maidenhair)

suitability   *
beginner   *

Comments
Ancient species with fossil specimens found from the age of the dinosaurs. Mainly grown for interest only.

Ilex (holly)

suitability   ***
beginner   **

Comments
Sharp, pointed leaves, but can be turned into good Bonsai.

Juniperus (juniper)

Dozens readily available including:
J. chinensis (Chinese juniper), *J. media* (many varieties), *J. rigida* (needle juniper), *J. communis* (common juniper) and *J. squamata*.

suitability   *****
beginner   *****

Comments
One of the best shrubs for Bonsai. Most have small needle-like juvenile foliage when young, but this gives way to an attractive, scale-like texture as they age. Particularly good for dead wood effects and styles. Needle juniper is slightly more demanding.

Larix (larch)

suitability   *****
beginner   ****

Comments

Widely available and easy
to train.

Ligustrum (privet)

suitability   **
beginner   ***

Comments

Easy to grow and very
tolerant.

Lonicera (honeysuckle)

L. nitida (dwarf
honeysuckle) is the only
honeysuckle with merits for
Bonsai.

suitability   ***
beginner   ***

Comments

Tiny leaves, but slow-
growing.

Malus (crab apple)

suitability   ***
beginner   **

Comments

Invariably badly grafted.
A short-trunked example
with an unobtrusive graft
is worth using for Bonsai.

Picea (spruce)

suitability   ****
beginner   ****

Comments

Tiny needles, quite tough.
Well worth using.

Pinus (pine)

Many classic species
including:
P. mugo (mountain pine),
P. pentaphylla (white pine),
P. thunbergii (black pine),
and best of all P. sylvestris
(Scots pine).

suitability   *****
beginner   ****

Comments

Pines are, perhaps, the best
of all trees for Bonsai. Most
are not difficult to keep, but
some knowledge of their
growth habits is needed to
get the best from them in
the long term.

Populus (poplar)

suitability   *
beginner   *

Comments

Columnar growth habit not
well suited to Bonsai
training.

Prunus (cherry and apricot)

suitability   ***
beginner   ***

Comments

P. mume in particular makes
superb literati Bonsai.

Pyracantha (firethorn)

suitability   ***
beginner   ****

Comments

Widely available. Many
varieties have thorns.
Flowers and fruit are
attractive.

Quercus (oak)

suitability   ***
beginner   **

Comments

Prone to mildew and does
not like to be excessively
root-pruned. But a
wonderful genus, and
worth trying.

Rhododendron (and Azalea)

suitability   ****
beginner   ****

Comments

Wide availability; lovely
flowers; many dwarf
varieties adapt well to Bonsai
training. Many have fairly
brittle branches.
Rhododendrons and azaleas
need acid soil conditions.

Salix (willow)

suitability   ***
beginner   *****

Comments

Weeping style easily
achieved. Any pieces cut
from a willow tree will
readily root if you just
place them in water for a
few weeks. Satisfyingly
easy to achieve a Bonsai
from nothing in a short
space of time.

Sequoia (redwood)

Including related genera
Sequoiadendron and
Metasequoia.

suitability   ***
beginner   ***

Comments

Develops superb root
buttress and taper in little
time. Specimens already
exhibiting these
characteristics are sometimes
found at garden outlets.
Looks best when styled into
its natural mature shape of a
tall tapering tree with
drooping branches.

Taxus (yew)

suitability   ****
beginner   ****

Comments

Roots must be kept frost-
free in winter. Avoid
fastigiate varieties. Look
for the female plant which
bears the familiar attractive
red berries.

Thuja

suitability   *
beginner   **

Comments

Popular garden conifer,
marginally better for Bonsai
than Chamaecyparis.

Tsuga (hemlock)

suitability   ***
beginner   ***

Comments

Worth trying.

Ulmus (elm)

suitability   *****
beginner   ****

Comments

Best species are U. parvifolia
(Chinese elm) - which has
very small leaves, and U.
procera (English elm).

Wisteria

suitability   ***
beginner   **

Comments

Grown for the wonderful
racemes of flowers, but
getting it to actually flower
can be difficult.

Zelkova (Japanese grey-barked elm)

suitability   *****
beginner   ****

Comments

Simple to grow. Most often
used for broom-style Bonsai,
but suitable for many
other styles.

153

Locating suppliers of Bonsai materials

There are nurseries specializing in supplying Bonsai trees and materials. For example, in the UK there are over twenty, and in the USA more than fifty. It is not practicable to give an exhaustive list of these nurseries as any information may be out of date by the time this is read. However, an excellent method of locating your nearest supplier is to order your own country's Bonsai magazine. Ask your newspaper or magazine supplier for a copy of a magazine with Bonsai in its title. Many Bonsai nurseries and materials suppliers will appear in the advertisements section. The majority will happily supply goods by mail order.

Here are two addresses of Bonsai magazines that contain advertisements for material suppliers:-

Bonsai
Esco Business Service
FREEPOST
Finchingfield
Braintree
Essex CM7 4BR
United Kingdom

Bonsai Today
P.O. Box 816
Sudbury
MA 01776
USA

Clubs and societies

There are Bonsai clubs and societies in almost every country. Joining a club is a good way of meeting fellow enthusiasts and learning more about the hobby. Many have guest speakers and organize trips to Bonsai nurseries. A current magazine will list addresses.

The following are useful addresses of national organizing societies who will be able to advise you of your nearest club or society. It is always a good idea to enclose a stamped addressed envelope along with your enquiry.

UK
Federation of British Bonsai Clubs (FOBBS)
14 Somerville Road
Sutton Coldfield
West Midlands B73 6JA
United Kingdom

Australia
Bonsai Society of Australia
29 Beattie Road
Ryde 2112
Australia

USA
American Bonsai Society
P.O. Box 1136
Puyallup, WA
98371-1136
USA

World-wide
Bonsai Clubs International
2636 W. Mission Road #277
Tallahassee
Florida 32304-2556
USA

Primaeval forest ... or a Bonsai enthusiast letting loose his imagination?

A final few words...

Throughout this book the emphasis has been on active participation. Bonsai is a practical subject not a theoretical one, and to get the most from it requires a degree of enthusiastic involvement. The hardest aspect of teaching the skills of creating Bonsai is that the most important ingredient, the living plant material, is always variable. In a pursuit such as painting, the teacher knows that the materials his students use are largely the same the world over, but the Bonsai teacher must second-guess all the multitude of variations of plant materials and try to accommodate their differences within the instructional exercises. In one volume it is, of course, impossible to cover all the myriad possibilities, so the focus of this book has been on simplification through the use of practical example. At the end of the day, the Bonsai student will invariably have to use common sense and initiative to resolve the challenges posed by the subject.

Let me finish with a few items of review and summary, and a few additional tips.

Be bold with your Bonsai. They require a sensitive hand but will only develop into 'little trees' if you shape them that way.

Copy Nature. The trees in the wild are there to be appreciated by all and to be used as role models by the designer of Bonsai trees.

Search for the best-quality material you can find. Quality material usually gives quality results. Try to find material growing in the wild - it has characteristics that are not found in nursery-grown trees.

Pay attention to detail. Bonsai are small and all mistakes and poor workmanship stand out. Poor wiring techniques and unsealed cuts are not the mark of an artist - they indicate a lack of pride in one's workmanship.

Look at Bonsai. Visit exhibitions and Bonsai nurseries, subscribe to a magazine. Get ideas for your own Bonsai from those you admire.

If you have enjoyed this book, then please recommend it to your friends - share your knowledge of the hobby with others.

Above all else - enjoy your Bonsai !

Glossary

Apex
The top or summit of a Bonsai; the highest part above the root system.

Asymmetry
Lack of symmetry.

Branch-pruners
A Bonsai tool used for pruning branches, which leaves a concave impression.

Capillary action
Physical phenomenon whereby liquids may travel against the direction of gravity through minute connected spaces.

Chelated iron
A chemical contained in some fertilizers and plant conditioning treatments that helps the absorption of iron and prevents chlorosis in lime-hating plants.

Chlorosis
Yellowing of leaves on lime-hating plants such as azalea due to an excess of lime in the soil. It is treated by application of a fertilizer or tonic containing chelated iron.

Compound leaf
A leaf which has several smaller leaflets.

Dai
Hand crafted wooden stand for a viewing stone.

Deciduous
(Of a tree or shrub) annually shedding leaves.

En Mag
A proprietary chemical fertilizer high in magnesium.

Ericaceous
Usually applies to ericaceous composts that are lime free.

Evergreen
Keeping leaves all year round.

Fastigiate
Growth pattern of some plants which is profusely upwards-dominant.

Humidity
The amount of water vapour in the atmosphere.

Internode
Distance on a plant stem between sets of buds.

Jin
Japanese word for a dead branch.

Lime sulphur
Chemical composition of lime and sulphur which is applied to dead wood areas of Bonsai to bleach and preserve the wood.

Mycorrhiza
Beneficial fungus that forms a symbiotic relationship with plant roots.

Netlon
Plastic netting used for screening and providing shade.

Osmosis
Passage of liquid solutions through a membrane such as a root wall.

Penjing
Chinese form of landscape planting.

Photosynthesis
Biological process whereby plants convert carbon dioxide and water in the presence of light into food (sugars) and oxygen.

Ramification
Dense, twiggy branch structure.

Rootage
The root buttress at the base of the trunk.

Shari
Japanese word for a portion of the trunk with the bark removed.

Suiseki
Japanese word for the study of Viewing Stones.

Symbiosis
Relationship between two different organisms for their mutual benefit.

Taper
Vertical narrowing of the trunk.

Tokonoma
Small alcove at the entrance to Japanese homes where Bonsai are displayed.

Transpiration
Loss of water through the leaves of a plant.

Vine weevil
The larvae of this beetle feed off roots and are quite resilient. Can be eradicated with Gamma-HCH.

Wound sealant
Special paste applied to cuts on branches and trunks to assist healing.

Credits

All photographs have been taken by the author, who is not a professional photographer and who has struggled with a tangle of lights, cameras, lenses and all the other paraphernalia of photography !

All the Bonsai featured are from the author's collection - both past and present.

Acknowledgements

I would like sincerely to thank the following for their generous assistance: Jean Price and Pat Davies for editing, and verifying the flow and continuity of the book; Dick Maidment for providing 'another pair of hands' and proof-reading; Timothy Auger of B.T. Batsford Ltd, the publishers, for helping me to realize my goal of a pictorial approach to teaching the skills and techniques of Bonsai; Peter Adams and Dan Barton for originally opening my eyes to Bonsai as an art form.

My appreciation goes to Dave Cooper for his advice on photography, loan of the lights, and proof-reading. My gratitude is due to Jill Jonas for all the work she has put into testing the viability of the projects. I am indebted to my good friend Dave Sampson for his suggestions, constructive criticism and enthusiastic support.

But most of all I would like to thank my wife Lesley, for her tolerance, patience, understanding, and loyalty over the years that I have engaged in Bonsai as a vocation. Without her support I would never have achieved my goal of this treatise on Bonsai.

Index

159

WILBRAHAM PUBLIC LIBRARY

WILBRAHAM PUBLIC LIBRARY